S0-AGW-491

DISCARD

A HISTORY OF

CHOWDER

An ocean quahog. *United States Fish Commission (1872).*

A HISTORY OF

CHOWDER

FOUR CENTURIES OF

A NEW ENGLAND MEAL

Robert S. Cox & Jacob Walker

Charleston ┠─┨ London

THE
History
PRESS

Published by The History Press
Charleston, SC 29403
www.historypress.net

Copyright © 2011 by Robert S. Cox and Jacob Walker
All rights reserved

Cover design by Julie Scofield

Front cover: Chowder on the marsh. A Woll family pot.

All photographs are by Jacob Walker unless otherwise noted.

First published 2011

Manufactured in the United States

ISBN 978.1.60949.259.5

Library of Congress Cataloging-in-Publication Data

Cox, Robert S.
A history of chowder : four centuries of a New England meal / Robert S. Cox
and Jacob Walker
p. cm.
Includes bibliographical references.
ISBN 978-1-60949-259-5
1. Stews--New England--History. 2. Soups--New England--History. 3. Cooking
(Fish) 4. Cooking (Shellfish) 5. Cooking, American--New England style. I. Cox,
Robert S., 1958- II. Title.
TX693.W368 2011
641.5974--dc23
2011017901

Notice: The information in this book is true and complete to the best of our
knowledge. It is offered without guarantee on the part of the author or The
History Press. The author and The History Press disclaim all liability in
connection with the use of this book.

All rights reserved. No part of this book may be reproduced or transmitted in any
form whatsoever without prior written permission from the publisher except in
the case of brief quotations embodied in critical articles and reviews.

For those who chose the sea

Contents

Chowder in Preparation

In the mid-twelfth century in a Benedictine monastery in the Rhine region of Germany, Hildegard of Bingen, a polymath, wrote up a recipe and a cure. It was an ointment for the skin, a treatment for ulcers—a mixture of whale brain and water, boiled and mashed with goutweed and oil. It was not her only prescription. Hildegard's work on the natural sciences, *Physica*, contained many: Place the fish's eyelids in wine overnight and drink warm; a paralyzed tongue will come untied. Grind its bones with water and feed it to the pigs; the plague will fade. Her powerful remedies are not meals. They are not testaments to early chowder making found far from the New England shoreline, just reminders of simple importance. The world over, playing with fish, fat and water has long been a part of our humanity.

Time and place may make the creative aspirations of New England cooks more appealing than Bingen's (they are), but in essence we are up to the same tricks. Today, the restorative properties of food can be sidelined in favor of celebrations of certain ingredients or exercises in overeating. Chowder, however, carries on its good work. It can be part of the way to live a better life here. If all our references to chowder were to vanish, many might collapse into despair. In 1885, a man in Roxbury, Massachusetts, wrote, "Chowder is probably the form of nourishment which most quickly and easily comes to the restoration or refreshment of the brain of man." Maybe he was right.

The progress of chowder eating is different for each of us. For some, the initial taste may be had as a young child, a response to years of eating from jars of fruits and vegetables. A spoonful of chowder may be given to us by our parents, or we may order a bowl to mirror them. For those holding an aversion to an ingredient it can take time. A friend of mine did not have chowder till age twenty. Another hesitates: the broth is a reminder of mayonnaise. But for those on track, each chowder strengthens the ability to distinguish the good from the bad. In our patterns of eating we each string up sets of different bowls—preferences brought by circumstance and expectation. Some may enjoy cream chowders their whole lives and never sway from the habit. Others may jump between the milk and the water and find themselves never liking clams over cod or corn over haddock. Pulling at this line can bring any bowl back.

A middle-aged couple dining by the Cape Cod Canal finished up two plates of fish and chips before going on their way. I placed an order and took a seat as the air came through the door closing behind them. A bowl of chowder and fritters came to the table. Grease poured through the bag. I dumped in a packet of crackers and ate it, then used a napkin. There was an employee in his twenties sitting a table away. He was having a hot dog and reading the paper on a break. He complained about the last shift. He was looking for a new job. We talked about chowder. He asked, "Is it really from New England?"

Chowder Begins

For New Englanders, and those who would be ones, chowder is a sea swell of the soul. A bowl of chowder (never a cup) evokes a forgotten day years ago, a slanted shaft of light on a wooden table, a stove-top pot steaming as the languorous hours of an autumn afternoon drift toward revelation. Chowder recalls a breeze-swept shore, a celebration of friends and walkers-by decked out in rain gear and wool, seasoned with salt and sand and shocks of briny kelp. For Henry David Thoreau, chowder was the culmination of a day in his beloved Concord woods; for Herman Melville, it sang of the friendship of unlikely shipmates discovering the "fishiest of all fishy places," a weathered tavern in the byways of Nantucket. A simmering bowl, a shore-side meal, chowder is sustenance in its most elemental form—sustenance of body and mind—a marker of hearth and home, community, family and culture. So many liquid shades of recall, chowder charts the shoals and eddies of the New England shore and points the way home.

This simple dish—this simple congeries of simple things, cooked simply—is so basic that it is tempting to say what it is not rather than what it is. It is not, for example, a dish for the refined of palate, a bowl for the finicky, the fancy or fussy. It is neither the dainty fare of the elite nor some exotic swaddling thing newly arrived on our national doorstep. It is no adventurous foray into the nether regions of the food chain. Chowder shuns the aesthetic and the summery challenge of spice and heat in favor of wintry grays and whites. It opts for savory over sweet, a layered pot over layered flavor. Salt and pepper, potatoes and onion, pork and fish, cream and hard crackers—there is nothing nouvelle here.

If chowder is elegant, then, it is only so in its simplicity, in its assertive lack of assertiveness. Yet somehow, these scant half dozen ingredients combined have cast a spell over generations of New Englanders. For all its unassuming nature, chowder is defended as fiercely in the region as any national dish has ever been by any ravenous horde. Ask a Red Sox fan about the Yankees, or the Patriots about the Jets, and you will receive a taste of what New Englanders feel about the degenerate soup endemic to Manhattan. New Englanders are bred in the bone with a favorite joint, a favored recipe and a revered chowder master. It is our legacy, our collective memory. In all its varied forms, it is a dish of proportion, substance and balance and can no more be reduced to just another seafood stew than a fine French bread can be reduced to a mere sum of flour, salt, yeast and water. For New Englanders, it has become more than a dish. In its simplest forms, and most elaborate, it is to the region as the madeleine was to Marcel Proust—a way of remembering and experiencing a common past, and sometimes creating it.

Food, as the anthropologist Mary Douglas has written, is so much more than the sum of nutrition, economics and taste; it penetrates deeply into the "moral and social intentions of individuals," shaping the world as we know it and defining our relations with others. Our beliefs and practices about food (foodways, to use the anthropological term) bring our peculiar notions about our culture into high relief, symbolically representing what we hold close to the heart and what we reject as beyond the pale. Joining together in the preparation, cooking and sharing of meals and memories helps us to see and sense the most intimate bonds that unite us. It clarifies the values we share and our particular roles within our circle of family and friends and the community at large. A simple phrase like "break bread" surpasses the words themselves; it conjures a world of relationships, a new sense of the emotional and personal expectations that connect us. To keep kosher, to eat vegan, to say grace and even to reheat a TV dinner in the microwave is cultural shorthand for much deeper sets of commitments, and which course we follow in our cuisine reveals as much about us as consumers—as family or community—as volumes of ethnography ever can. Every action has its significance to the cook and consumer, whether separating meat from dairy or peeling back the plastic cover from a plastic tray.

Foodways, in fact, may be among the most important means by which the members of a community come to understand their place in the world. As food historians Etta M. Madden and Martha L. Finch write, foodways are the means by which people "achieve their ideals" and then "display those ideals to themselves and outsiders." In the modern United States, where a meal can be little more than a thin sandwich in the vacant hours of an afternoon, the act of sitting around a table together, breaking bread, becomes a powerful statement about those we love and those who love us. This is what we long for, what we value; this is who we are.

Madden and Finch argue that foodways resonate in four distinct registers. Symbolically, foodways represent and communicate the values dear to us and our community. Functionally, they help create bonds within and around a community, providing a means of material and ideological negotiation with the outside world. Mnemonically, they connect our past to our present and future, creating the impression of an unbroken chain. Finally, dynamically, foodways enact and reflect change in a community's social values. In these ways, a simple meal can evoke subtle and even conflicting sets of meanings. For some Brazilians, as Madden and Finch note, eating a quarter pounder with cheese at McDonalds may reflect "the displacement of local values and practices by U.S. imperialism," but at another seat in the same restaurant, other Brazilians might imagine themselves "symbolically ingesting all they see as positive about the United States." Foodways, according to Madden and Finch, "help members continuously create a particular world and define their relations to the larger world in which they live."

Symbolically, functionally, mnemonically or dynamically, as we will see, chowder has become a powerful means for New Englanders to define themselves as a community, a rich community with a deep past and values that distinguish our region from all others. And yet, chowder suggests a strange thing about New England. While the dish has long been made here, while it has a close association with our people and climate, it only became entrenched in our souls when that feeling of community began to fray. And peril is a feeling long familiar to the New England mind. Even while the Puritans held political and social sway here, they feared that New England had fallen away from its founding ideals, from the tightly knit social fabric that our earliest immigrants had so carefully woven. In the generation of Cotton Mather—and often since—New England ministers railed against our declension from godly purity and social unity, and a century later, writers like Harriet Beecher Stowe picked up the thread, yearning for a New England before the coming of the telegraph and rail, before steam power and steam-powered ideas changed our moral fiber.

In her novel *Oldtown Folks*, Stowe remembered the days of that New England past, when the residents of hamlets and villages from the Atlantic shore to the Berkshire Hills lived as "part and parcel," she wrote, "of a great picture of the society in which he live[d] and act[ed]." She was convinced that those times were evaporating in the harsh sunlight of the modern day. Through her writing, she sought to cling to those "ante-railroad times," the old times when "our own hard, rocky, sterile New England was a sort of half Hebrew theocracy, half ultra-democratic republic of little villages, separated by a pathless ocean from all the civilization and refinement of the Old World, forgotten and unnoticed, and yet burning like live coals under this obscurity with all the fervid activity of an intense, newly kindled, peculiar, and individual life." Those times were already gone, or nearly so, and she longed for that pure and simple past:

> For that simple, pastoral germ-state of society is a thing forever gone. Never again shall we see that union of perfect repose in regard to outward surroundings and outward life with that intense activity of the inward and intellectual world, that made New England, at this time, the vigorous, germinating seed-bed for all that has since been developed of politics, laws, letters, and theology, through New England to America, and through America to the world. The hurry of railroads, and the rush and roar of business that now fill it, would have prevented that germinating process. It was necessary that there should be a period like that we describe, when villages were each a separate little democracy, shut off by rough roads and forests from the rest of the world, organized round the church and school as a common centre, and formed by the minister and the schoolmaster.

In a society in which the bonds of community are maintained largely by face-to-face contact, nostalgia is unnecessary, but as those intimacies fade, a yearning for the symbols of the past gnaws deep into the psyche. Chowder is just one of those symbols to which New Englanders attached themselves; just as some were drawn to the ancient houses and small villages of the colonial revival movement and others cleaved themselves to the imagined arts and crafts of an imagined past, so many New Englanders have reached for the chowder pot and the olden recipes that sustained their forefathers. This is not nostalgia, though it is like it. Chowder plays a pivotal role in creating a sense of community through the fierce defense of the "true" or "authentic" and through the implicit meanings of simple ingredients prepared with special care in a special way. Chowder evokes what Madden and Finch call the "visceral memories that provide feelings of familiarity, comfort, and continuity," and the rituals surrounding its consumption— the chowder party—provide an opportunity to learn what it is to behave like a proper New Englander and to show who we are. It is the ultimate comfort food: it is comfort food for a culture.

A chowder supper on the coast with a plate of crackers and bottles of fresh milk and cream.

Harriet Beecher Stowe knew about chowder, but as we shall see, the history of this simple and essential dish became the past that generations of New Englanders imagined, even as it gained a foothold in the present and a place for the future.

CHOWDER HAS AN IDENTITY

As a general proposition, a history of the Reformation ought to begin with a proper discussion of just what was being reformed, and if we were to set our sights on writing about a revolution, we might well wish to know who was revolting. In the same vein, it would be a fine idea to begin a discussion of chowder with an introduction to where it originated and what it is. That we will not provide. As it turns out, neither reforming the western religious tradition nor casting off the shackles of tyranny present a problem quite as thorny as the chowder pot. Chowder simply defies any logic but its own. Through time, the dish has metamorphosed from rough-hewn shipboard roots into versions fitted out for more refined, though seldom genteel, tables. Subtly but surely, the ingredients have evolved through time, as has the manner in which they are handled and the manner in which they are received, and even within New England itself, different regions have followed their own chowdery paths, with some, like wayward Connecticut, venturing too far for many would-be purists and others hewing close to the trunk of the ancestral tree. To define what chowder is turns out to be not such an easy task.

To be sure, there are some distinctive aspects of chowder that have barely changed through the years. The earliest published recipe for the dish, a poetical piece published in the *Boston Evening Post* on September 23, 1751, is very much recognizable as a chowder, even to modern eyes, though it might look and taste like a distant relative to the modern palate:

First lay some Onions to keep the Pork from burning,
Because in chouder there can be no turning;
Then lay some Pork in slices very thin,
This you in Chouder always must begin.
Next lay some Fish oer crossways very nice
Then season well with Pepper, Salt and Spice;
Parsley, Sweet-Marjoram, Savory and Thyme,
Then Biscuit next which must be soak'd some Time.
Thus your Foundation laid, you will be able
To raise a chouder, high as Tower of Babel;
For by reapeating o'er the Same again,
You may make Chouder for a thousand Men.
Last Bottle of Claret, with Water eno' to smother 'em,
You'l have a Mess which some call Omnium gather 'em.

Like most early chowders, the *Post* dish was thick and layered. Starting with a base of salt pork rendered to provide fat and flavor, and onions to lend zest, it climbed through as many strata of fish and biscuit as the pot would allow before being doused with just enough water to cover the whole. Herbs of various sorts, wine or occasionally other flavorings could be added to the pot to lend a little kiss, but every bowl was a hefty bowl, even without two of the ingredients that define chowder for most New Englanders today: potato and milk. And then there were the clams. More about these later. Surprisingly, throughout the history of chowder, the only ingredients common to all—or nearly all—are salt pork (or its equivalent) and to a lesser degree onions. Even these lonely chorus players cannot always be relied upon.

In twentieth-century kitchens, the unruly tides of New England chowder have carved out a handful of discrete channels. Although cookbook writers enjoy nothing more than to concoct new and exotic chowders, the more traditional varieties of the dish differ in a mere handful of seemingly innocuous decisions relating to only a handful of ingredients: whether or not they contain dairy, whether potatoes or other vegetables are involved, whether the main protein is fish or shellfish and whether herbs or other add-ins are included. Where one comes from, it seems, says much about how a person decides what is proper. Chowder is regional. The most famous interloper, the tomato, began littering stewpots in southern New England as early as the 1870s, and since that time, it has become characteristic of that impoverished cuisine. In Maine, lobster bodies may be used to flavor the broth; New Hampshirites traditionally disdain vegetables altogether, while Rhode Islanders shun the dairy; and although the first splash of milk took a while to be accepted, it is now de rigueur in Massachusetts and at many points spreading out from there.

While the white, milk-based chowder of Massachusetts is often set apart from the tomato- and vegetable-laden Manhattan style, strange hybrids can be found. Along the I-91 corridor, tomato and milk sometimes combine to make a bright pink potage that seems to please no one but the confused remnants who live in that thin band between Sox and Yankees. In the dark estaminets of Providence and Pawtucket, a brothy bowl of Rhode Island chowder may sometimes be found flirting with a glass of milk for mixing in, and while early chowder makers made do with whatever fish might be at hand (though cod and haddock were most often preferred), modern chowders venture into scallops, clams, mussels and lobster and even into non-seafood, like the vaguely sinister cheeseburger chowder. Within their seemingly tight constraints, chowder masters can be surprisingly innovative, as they have been for centuries. The chowder pot has limited hues, but it is a palate to be admired.

It is perhaps easiest to think of regional tastes in modern chowder by reference to the science of epidemiology: distinct tastes radiate outward from three distinct centers of infection. From the western Connecticut shore, the tomato has spread

A shanty used for shucking clams showing the results of six weeks of steady digging. *A Report from the Mollusk Fisheries of Massachusetts (1909).*

coastwise to the Rhode Island border; dairy has spread outward from Boston Harbor to nearly every corner of the chowder world; while the brothy variants have held on in the vicinity of Narragansett Bay. In the end, however, the variations in chowder making within a region are often greater than the variation between regions, confounding expectations left and right. For all the disdain heaped upon the tomato, that fruit has a long New England history, and blaming it on (or crediting it to) Italian immigrants in New York and their zuppa di pesce seems unnecessary, given that the tomato has been part of Connecticut cuisine since prior to the great wave of Italian immigration.

What, then, makes a chowder? The great food writer John Thorne has both begged the question and offered a key insight. For him, chowder "represents the special preparation of some very ordinary ingredients, while a stew represents an ordinary preparation of some very special ingredients." To a native New Englander, a gourmet chowder is as offensive to the sensibilities as a gourmet cheese steak is to a native Philadelphian (delicious offense, but offense nonetheless). This is a plain dish, pure and simple—more substantial than a typical soup, more unassuming than a hearty stew. With that in mind, let us wander from the colonial coast to the New England present.

CHOWDER AND THE NEWFOUND LANDS

Early in the eighteenth century, the word chowder became firmly affixed to one of the myriad seaside soups of the North Atlantic rim, a soup that was closely associated with the vast fishing grounds along the continent's northeastern margin. Sadly, no one at the time saw fit to record the momentous occasion when word met dish, and no one thought to comment on where either soup or saying originated. Perhaps it seemed all too obvious at the time, or too banal, or perhaps faintness from the call of hunger drowned out the fainter urge to write, but for whatever reason, writing a history of a humble soup was on no one's top ten list of things to do in the year 1732. The disinterest of our forefathers, however, has done little to quell the appetites of modern food writers, who for years have spilled gallons of ink on reams of paper in attempts to divine who concocted the first bowl. They do so at their own peril. The first mistake of any historian, of course, is to claim a first for anything, and for several reasons, to speak of the first bowl of chowder may just be fishing for trouble.

In the colonial era, the Atlantic rim was home to countless variations on the theme of seafood soup, and it has tempted more than one writer to point to one particular soup or another as the Adam to our chowdery Eve. Quite often, writers have pointed to France as its particular paradise. The French phrase *faire la chaudière* has been the favored starting point for many discussions, thanks to the *Oxford English Dictionary*, and when spoken like a pirate, *chaudière* does indeed sound remarkably like our favorite meal. The etymologists of the venerable *OED* certainly thought so, citing an authority from 1871 who claimed that cabarets in obscure fishing villages in Brittany still hung signs that read, "Ici on fait la chaudière"—or "here be chowder" (in pirate speak). According to this author, *faire la chaudière* meant "to supply a cauldron in which is cooked a mess of fish and biscuit with some savoury condiments, a hodge-podge contributed by the fishermen themselves, each of whom in return receives his share of the prepared dish." The story goes that the word *chaudière*, sometimes translated as "cauldron," eventually became attached to the meal within, and when conveyed across the Atlantic by fishermen—perhaps even by the noted explorer Jacques Cartier himself—that dish found fertile grounds, spreading out over the cod-rich banks of Newfoundland and from there down the coast of Nova Scotia to the heartland of New England.

Nor is the *OED* alone in its musings on French origins. In 1890, a contributor to the periodical *American Notes and Queries* added a uniquely American twist to the story, recalling an incident in which the poet Henry Wadsworth Longfellow allegedly surprised a French visitor with the news that chowder was a French invention. According to the alleged Longfellow's alleged story, French settlers in Canada may not actually have brought the dish with them like so many gate crashers at a colonial potluck, but once they settled here, "Mother Necessity soon taught them how to stew clams and fish in layers with bacon, sea biscuits and other ingredients in a kettle (Chaudière)." Chowder, in other words, was a force of nature imposed upon the French, who seem to be genetically prone to culinary innovation. From here, Indians enter the story (to make it truly an American dish), and "when they heard the Gaul speak of the Chaudière," the alleged Longfellow continued, they "supposed it referred to the food," calling it something like "chawder." From there, our rock-ribbed Yankees entered the scene to corrupt the words further,

A New England boathouse covered with buoys, nets and oars. *Courtesy of D.W.*

and Americanize them more, so that at the end of this colonial version of the telephone game, generations of Yankee tongues would ever after repeat "chowder."

Suspicions of French origins, then, are widely shared, and to be sure, they sound plausible. Who would deny a Frenchman his soup? But neither history nor historians are always so tidy, and there are reasons to question, if not doubt, the story. Food historian John Thorne, for one, has observed that the French word for cauldron is *chaudron*, while *chaudière* is reserved for something more akin to a steam boiler—a rather significant difference given the way chowder is actually prepared. Furthermore, Thorne notes, French food historians—"who do not usually duck such credit"—have never claimed patrimony for chowder. To put the nail in the coffin, Thorne adds that the Breton soup *chaudrée* (so close in sound to our beloved dish) is no more or less like New England chowder than any number of other Atlantic fish stews. They may sound alike, and may share some tasty fish, but that hardly makes them brothers.

Unfortunately for our cause, the writers who deviate from the story of French origins are just as interesting, and just as dubious. In his excellent history of cod, Mark Kurlansky looks to the Celtic fringe of Great Britain, rather than France, for the ancestor to our beloved soup, citing an intriguing sixteenth-century recipe for chowder written in the Cornish language, noting that the Cornish word for fishmonger is *jowter*. It hardly takes a pirate to hear the homophone. But Kurlansky also adds that Native Americans in the Northeast were already making chowder prior to arrival of Europeans, though without the pork—which, of course, would make it not chowder, or at least no more chowder than a dozen other fish stews. Close in seafood soup is just not close enough.

We may never settle the question, but there may also be a good reason for our failure to do so. Long before the first wave of European settlement in North America, the Atlantic was a cauldron of tongues and taste buds. Nearly one hundred years before the Pilgrims landed at Plymouth Rock, John Rut wrote that when his ship sailed into the harbor at St. Johns, Newfoundland, he "found eleven sails of Normans, and one Brittaine, and two Portugall Barkes, and all a-fishing." In the 1600s, a Basque fisherman plying his trade on Georges Bank or the Grand Banks might have more readily encountered Frenchmen, Spaniards or Englishmen there than at home, and he would have surely run into the Passamaquoddys, Micmacs or Penobscots; Africans; West Indians; and perhaps an odd Dutchman, Swede or Dane.

At sea, it was men—most often only men—wherever you looked, but whether blue-water sailing or coastwise trade, life at sea was a constant encounter of races and languages. In early America, the polyglot crews were assembled where they could be had, in homeports and foreign. They were recruited from young boys and wizened old hands, from rascals and rabble, drifters and adventurers, the fortunate and unfortunate in life, fortune seekers and fortune takers. Naval, fishing, whaling and trading ships each had their own unique cultures and flavors, but all faced a rigorous reality. Tossed about in tiny wooden ships through leagues of rough North Atlantic weather, crews faced the perils of contagious disease and scurvy and the possibility of failure on each leg of every journey, along with the daily dangers of hooks, knives and nets on roiling seas and rolling decks, all while confined to a world framed in oak and measured in a few dank feet. This was a crude and intimate world, a world where Queequeg and Ishmael shared bunks and could hardly be out of sight of each other for months at a time.

Make no mistake about it, food was an essential part of this world. If an army travels on its stomach, a ship sails by its bowels. Limited by what could be packed into a ship's small larder, restricted by what foodstuffs could survive the damp conditions and lack of refrigeration without spoilage and constrained by what could be obtained at sea or on visits to port, a sailor's diet was often monotonous, seldom adventurous, but always essential. A cook aboard even a small ship might come from a different town, a different region or different nation from his fellow seamen, and each member of the crew brought his own natal tastes and expectations to the table. With all the intimate exchanges, the sharing of labors and hopes below decks and above, why would we expect that chowder originated at some discreet point or time? Fishermen, being fisherman, have sailed coastwise for centuries and crossed blue Atlantic water for the opposite shore since at least the time of Columbus, carrying with them the tastes of their distinctive homelands and stores of their favored ingredients, and they were necessarily adept at exploiting whatever they could harvest, gather or barter for at sea to supplement their diet, making do with foods that would appeal just enough to the crew to keep them on this side of civility. Personal and national preferences were matched by the need for adaptability and even ingenuity, with or without Mother Nature's kind instruction.

Forecastle of a schooner, the setting for a supper at sea. *Etching by C.B. Hudson (1888).*

Perhaps it is easier to imagine the prehistory of chowder than to confirm it, but while we may never be able to say definitively who created the first bowl, we do have some firm sand under our feet on which to do our imagining. Whether French, Cornish or some other language, whether linguistic corruption or verbal purity is at stake, the word chowder has some distinctive connotations so deeply attached to it that the significance may easily be overlooked. Most obviously, it is worth reemphasizing that from its earliest days, chowder was recognized as a product of a deep maritime culture, and particularly the culture of fishermen and fishing ports. This was a sea-borne dish that made its way ashore, rather than vice versa, and it was created according to the stringent realities of shipboard life. In that sense, too, it was a distinctly masculine dish, prepared by men for men (and sometimes women), and it was consumed according the rough manners of the waves rather than the refined manners of home or town or the conventions of mixed company. Finally, chowder was specifically recognized for its unique association with the maritime culture of the great cod lands of the western North Atlantic. Although by the late eighteenth century, seamen could be found consuming chowder as far away as the Pacific, as William Beresford did in May 1786 (and shark chowder at that), for most early observers, the word chowder raised thoughts of Newfoundland and the lands rimming the fertile fields stretching from the Grand Banks to the Georges Banks.

Even in the earliest appearances of the word chowder, these associations are well established. The first recorded use of the word is sometimes said to have been in a private diary for June 1732, when the jurist Benjamin Lynde described a voyage across Massachusetts Bay. With the famed Boston Lighthouse ahead and both Cape Cod and Cape Ann within sight at the same time, he wrote plainly: "Dined on a fine chowdered cod which the Captain caught." Lynde may have been no prose stylist, but there is a hint here of something, even if we must verge into the realm of speculation. It is noteworthy that Lynde used chowder as an adjective, not a noun, hinting, perhaps, that chowder originally might have referred as much to the method of preparation as the product prepared.

Stepping back a bit to look at the situation only adds to the mystery. In Lynde's day, and for three of four decades after, the word chowder was not reserved solely for fish stew, not even in its center of production. In fact, the word was applied just as often to another staple of Newfoundland: chowder beer. In his 1724 *General History of Pyrates* (published eight years prior to Lynde's passage), Charles Johnson explored why pirates thrived off the coast of Newfoundland, a "desolate and Woody" place that was held "only held for the Conveniency of the Cod Fishery." Thoughts of a Blackbeard fending off an angry cod-man with a cutlass may seem comical, but even at this early date criminals knew to go where the money was. Newfoundland attracted a diverse and lively criminal element to prey on the profits of a thriving triangular trade that linked their fish in a single economy with West Indian rum, molasses and sugar; durable goods from the Mediterranean; and slaves from Africa. This trade "accidentally contributes" to piracy, Johnson concluded, because the poor fellows who worked the cod boats—typically men from Devonshire and elsewhere in the West Country of England— were treated so harshly and paid such miserable wages that piracy seemed attractive by comparison. Once in Newfoundland, they were required to earn funds for their own passage home, Johnson wrote, and many suffered being stranded. The bitter northern winter left these young men with plenty of time to drink during long northern nights and little reason not to. They spent their time, according to Johnson, "drinking Black Strap, (a strong Liquor used there, and made from Rum, Molossus, and Chowder-Beer); by this the Majority of them out-run the Constable, and then are necessitated to come under hard Articles of Servitude for their Maintenance in the Winter." Piracy, where drunkenness was actively encouraged, looked better and better.

Clearly, by the time Johnson's book appeared in 1724, chowder beer must have been a familiar product, since the word (unlike blackstrap) required no further explanation. It was the beer that made St. Johns famous. Twenty years later, when the professional rascal Bampfylde-Moore Carew, "the noted Devonshire stroller and dog-stealer" (there is Devon again!) and self-styled "King of the Beggars," was looking for a false identity, his knowledge of Newfoundland came in handy. Cozying to his mark, Lady Mules, a woman with experience in the North Atlantic, Carew ripped off an "account of their Method of making their Chouder-Beer, and the Ingredients whereof it is made," turning her into putty in his hands. "This whimsical Gentlewoman," thereafter, "generously relieved and entertained him, and brought him a Cup of that Country Liquor which was of her own brewing." Score one for larceny and lies and another for native Newfoundland beers.

Also called spruce beer, chowder beer was widely popular during the eighteenth century, and although scarce today, it is still brewed by hard-core hobbyists and microbrewers in Canada. During the Seven Years' War, it was sometimes issued in regular rations to British troops in Canada, and it was proposed for use in the Royal Navy, where it was offered as a somewhat less damaging drink for seamen than the rum that was more commonly dispensed. Even more important, it was said to provide a preventive against scurvy or "the cure of it where it may have been contracted." A writer to the *London Magazine* for September 1764 provided a characteristic recipe:

METHOD OF PREPARING CHOWDER BEER

Take twelve gallons of water, and put therin three pounds and a half of black spruce. Boil it for three hours; then take out the fir, and put to the liquor seven pounds of melasses, and just boil it up. Then take it off, strain it through a sieve, and when milk is warm, put to it about four spoonfuls of yeast to work it.

For a common drink for seamen, two gallons of melasses may be sufficient to an hogshead of liquor. It soon works. In two or three days stop the bung in the cask, and in five or six days, when fine, bottle it for drinking…In the West-Indies they need boil but a trifle of the water; just enough to get the bitter out of the spruce. And two and a half gallons of melasses will make a hogshead of tolerable good drink. Good West-India melasses make better drink than treacle or coarse sugar; Though in the want of the former either of the others may serve.

The writer who supplied this recipe declared himself ignorant of the etymology of the word, speculating that it might be "a provincial phrase, known only in Devonshire," but it was a perfect drink for the expanding British empire, combining products produced in great abundance in the North American (spruce) and West Indian colonies (molasses) and preserving the health of the fleet wherever they roved by preventing the scourge of scurvy. Chowder beer made the empire stronger economically and militarily. It was both an intensely local drink and one that existed fundamentally on an Atlantic scale. Chowder beer, this self-identified merchant wrote, is "the wholesomest drink that is made; I am seldom without it when I can get spruce." He added that when he lived in New England and ran vessels to the West Indies and Honduras, he always made sure that his ship's master brought black spruce with him, noting that his crews never experienced the ill health from poor water that befell other merchantmen. "I have so great an opinion of the beer," he wrote, "that I wish it was used in all our ships on the coast of Guinea, and in the West-Indies; and where at many places the water is very bad." He continued:

Before the use of this beer was found at Newfoundland, the men were sickly, scorbutick, &c. but now no country where they are more healthy. I have heard a gentleman say, that now, when it has happened they had not the Chowder beer, for want of melasses to drink, they would be sick. I cannot but think it must be very beneficial to the sailors in general, who after they leave this country, likely the beer they carry from hence is expended in six weeks or two months; After that, if their voyage is twelve months or more, water is their common drink, which if good it might be tolerable; but at many places it is very bad, and at times, at sea, stinks, much in the casks. The beer that is carried to sea from hence seldom is racked, so that by the motion of the ships, after it is a little time in draught, it is very indifferent drink.

Brewed in the cod lands, chowder beer was part of an Atlantic empire that stretched from the American tropics to Africa and Britain. But such clues do little to resolve the question about where chowder originated or whether the term refers to some method of preparation common to beer and soup—perhaps the long simmering involved—or to some other property shared by both. We can only speculate on whether the term was transferred from beer to the soup or vice versa, or whether it attached to both beer and soup from another source entirely. We may never know. At this early stage, however, we can be confident that both products were born and embedded in the shipboard culture and both were clearly tied to Newfoundland. Perhaps it should not be surprising, but fish chowder and spruce beer were sometimes partners. From St. Johns, Newfoundland, William Boys (a survivor of a fire in 1727 aboard a slaveship) wrote, "They made chouder for us, and gave us a beer made of the tops of juniper, fermented with molasses."

Whatever its source, the word caught on in the popular culture of the British Atlantic world, appearing in novels and plays and bits of comic writing. As early as the 1760s, comic writers like Tobias Smollett used the term without further elaboration when drawing a caricature of a lusty seaman. In *The Adventures of Sir Launcelot Greaves*, Smollett introduced Crowe, a figure that spouts a steady spray of nautical jargon, ranting such things as: "Stop my hawse-holes…I can't think what's the matter, brother; but, agad, my head sings and simmers like a pot of chowder—My eye sight yaws to and again, d'ye see—then there's such a walloping and whushing in my hold—smite my—Lord have mercy upon us—Here, you swab, ne'er mind a glass—hand me the noggin." Nine years later, and a bit more cryptically, Smollett included a dog named Chowder in *The Expedition of Humphry Clinker*, a small and "filthy cur from Newfoundland," which was at times ailing, quarrelsome and constipated. Moving to the stage, in his comic play, *A Match for a Widow*, Joseph Atkinson relied on his audience's knowledge of colonial geography when introducing Jonathan, a character who announced that he was newly arrived from America, calling out that his master was "Captain Belmore—as good a man, I swear for it, as ever eat a cod's head and chowder!!" More authentically American he could not be.

And chowder was unmistakably American, growing in popularity as the eighteenth century wore on, appearing aboard ship and dock in the Revolutionary era and after with increasing frequency. In many cases, at least in those meriting special mention, chowder was associated with social gatherings, pleasant days aboard ship and gatherings of community and friends. Benjamin Lynde's chowdered cruise certainly had its social aspects, but Keith Stavely and Kathleen Fitzgerald cite an example a generation later that is more typical. Having gone to Boston in May 1760 to participate in the elections, the ministerial convention and Harvard College commencement, the Reverend

Ebenezer Parkman of Westborough, Massachusetts, cruised Boston Harbor with "a number of Gentlemen & Ladies," taking tea at the famed lighthouse (the same seen by Lynde) and on the return, the party "Eat our Chowder 'o board in good order." A little less elaborately, a few months before the Continental Congress declared its independence from Britain in 1776, Caleb Gannet, a minister and tutor at Harvard College, wrote that he and the college president ate "Shade Chowder at Capt. Heywood's Fish War [wharf]." Proving that soup takes no side, in August 1787, not long after the end of the Revolution, the British officer William Dyott described a military chowder feast in Nova Scotia (where Gannet had once preached), echoing hundreds of other chowder feasts over the centuries:

I went on a fishing party with Captain August Devernet of the artillery. It is one of the principal summer amusements of this place, and a very pleasant one indeed. There were ten of us; we had a large boat, allowed the artillery by government, and also a smaller one for the eatables. We set out about eleven o'clock, and sailed down the harbour to a place called the haddock bank, about two miles distance. We anchored and began to fish. Such astounding quantities of haddock I never saw. I believe in about one hour and a half we caught one hundred and fifty, and I took a large skate. The people have such a profusion of fish that they will scarce eat skate. When we had tired ourselves with fishing, we sailed to an island two miles lower down, where we landed; and as the principal thing in these parts is to eat chowder, we set the cooks to work to prepare dinner. A Mr. Roberts of the 57th regiment was to superintend the cooking the chowder. As it would necessarily take some time, Captain Devernet and I went into the woods to see if we could meet with any partridge, which are different in this country to what they are in England. They are found in woods, and perch upon the trees. The island we were upon is called Cornwallis Island, and was sold by the Bishop of Lichfield, Dr. Cornwallis, to a shoemaker of Halifax a few years ago. It contains about six hundred acres. There is but a small proportion of it cultivated at present. Wherever it has been at all cleared, it is astonishing what fine clover springs up spontaneously. The wood is chiefly birch and spruce fir. We did not venture far into the wood, it was so astonishingly hot, and the "moschetos" are very troublesome. Did not meet any game at all. On our return we found the table spread under the shade of a large birch and a fir, in a spot of about an acre, near a small cottage belonging to a poor fisherman, and close to the shore. The island formed a small bay in this place. The surrounding wood, which covered the hills on every side of the bay, and a most beautiful small island entirely covered with the spruce fir to the very water's edge about a league distance from the entrance of the bay, formed altogether a most beautiful prospect. We sat down about four o'clock, and of all the dishes I ever tasted, I never met so exquisitely good a thing as the chowder. We attempted to make it on board ship, but nothing like this. It is a soup, and better in my opinion than turtle. The recipe I don't exactly know, but the principal ingredients are cod and haddock, pork, onions, sea-biscuit, butter, and a large quantity of cayenne pepper. In short, the tout ensemble was the best thing I ever ate. We had some excellent Madeira, of which we drank a bottle each, and some very good lime punch with dinner. We rowed round the island, and returned home by nine o'clock. I never spent a more pleasant day. There are frequent parties of this kind.

For decades to come, a day of fishing, sailing and hunting in the woods, a pot of chowder and a bottle of wine made the perfect recipe for male bonding and, for many, a most pleasant day.

Cookbooks, Cod and Country

Outside the cod lands, the increasing familiarity with chowder may be partly attributable to the redoubtable Hannah Glasse, the English author of one of the most popular cookbooks of the eighteenth century. For decades, *The Art of Cookery Made Plain and Easy* was widely read on both sides of the Atlantic, and by the book's sixth edition in 1758, it offered a recipe for "Chouder, a Sea-dish":

> *Take a Belly-piece of pickled Pork, slice off the fatter Parts, and lay them at the Bottom of the Kettle, strew over it Onions, and such sweet Herbs as you can procure. Take a middling large Cod, bone and slice it as for Crimping, pepper, salt, allspice, and flour it a little, make a Layer with Part of the Slices; upon that a slight Layer of Pork again, and on that a Layer of Bisket, and so on, pursuing the like Rule, until the Kettle is filled to about four Inches; cover it with a nice Paste, pour in about a Pint of Water, lute down the Cover of the Kettle, and let the Top be supplied with live Wood-embers. Keep it over a slow Fire about four Hours.*
>
> *When you take it up, lay it in the Dish, pour in a Glass of hot Madeira Wine, and a very little India Pepper: If you have Oysters or Truffles, and Morels, it is still better; thicken it with Butter. Observe, before you put this Sauce in, to skim the Stew, and then lay on the Crust, and send it to Table reverse as in the Kettle; cover it close with the Paste, which should be brown.*

In these two brief paragraphs, Glasse laid out the core concept of eighteenth-century chowder: try some fatty salt pork in a kettle, fry some onions in the fat that renders out and then build layer upon layer of fish, pork and ship's biscuit before adding water, covering the pot and cooking slowly. The pork provided texture, richness and depth of flavor; the onions added zest; the fish ideally remained flaky and tasty; and the crackers—shipboard fare at its more basic—provided thickening. Published and republished over and again, Glasse's *Art of Cookery* influenced many other writers of cookbooks and, as far as one can guess, a generation of cooks. If imitation is the sincerest form of flattery, Glasse was flattered by many a pirate, not of the Devonish buccaneer kind, but of the literary kind in the days before copyright killed the quote. Richard Briggs, one of the most brazen brigands, reproduced Glasse's recipe almost verbatim under the heading "Directions for Sea-faring Men" in his book *The English Art of Cookery*, and many other writers parroted or paraphrased in similar fashion. Glasse's recipe became so familiar that her wording virtually became part of the definition of chowder. Literally. In the second edition of his *Classical Dictionary of the Vulgar Tongue* (1788), Francis Grose defined chowder in Glasse-like terms as "a sea dish, composed of fresh fish, salt pork, herbs, and sea-biscuits, laid in different layers, and stewed together."

It would be too much to say that published recipes helped standardize chowder making, for the simplicity of its construction allowed for a surprising number of subtle variations, and chowder evolved gradually as it made its way onto land. To begin with, different cooks had different preferences for their seafood. While many wrote that they preferred cod, haddock or sea bass, to name three of the fish most commonly cited, the enterprising shipboard cook made do with what was available, on land as at sea. As the accounts of Gannet, Dyott, Beresford and others suggest, hake would do in a pinch, as would bluefish, porgy, tutaug, mackerel, eel, sea bass, shad, skate and shark. Not that all fish were equally acceptable. Eliza Leslie, a Philadelphian and author of the most popular cookbook of the mid-nineteenth century, indicated that any good fish would do, but not halibut. "Halibut requires a much larger portion of seasoning, and a little more pork," she wrote. "Though very large and therefore very profitable, it is in itself the most tasteless of all fish. Plain boiled halibut is not worth eating."

Beyond her unexceptional choice in fish, Glasse's recipe is noteworthy in including subtle but significant additions to the chowder pot. Like many of the early published recipes, particularly those from cookbooks written by women, Glasse could not resist introducing a refining touch, and many later women followed with similar flourishes. Ashore, and unconstrained by stringent shipboard conditions, women (at least in cookbooks) introduced ingredients that would not have been available aboard fishing vessels of the day but that showed the cook's knowledge of the pantry and culinary skill, transforming a plain and hearty seaman's meal into a dish proper for the home. One might imagine a ship at sea carrying casks of Madeira, but the "Oysters or Truffles, and Morels" Glasse called for seem highly unlikely. More importantly, female writers transformed a workingman's dish into a domestic dish appropriate for the expectations placed on a middle-class American wife and mother. Indeed, most of the women who wrote cookbooks wrote in didactic mode, explicitly stating that they aimed to edify the young mother and women of lower social station but also to spread middle-class refinement, values and notions of womanhood. Whether their social lessers followed the lead of cookbook writers is difficult to gauge, but cookbooks were rife with advice.

In a sense, female cookbook writers made concerted efforts to domesticate chowder and bring it firmly within what was sometimes called the women's sphere. An obsession of lively advice literature during the early nineteenth century, the woman's sphere was based on the notion that women and men had distinctly different roles to play in society and different spheres within which they would operate. Women were imagined as being more emotional in nature, more nurturing, caring and spiritual, and they used those inherent traits to care for home and family and instruct their children in religious devotion. The men's sphere encompassed the world outside the home, participation in the workforce, the economy and politics, among other things. The doctrine of separate spheres provided women with a sense of mission and even a certain sense of social power in a world in which they were frequently denied rights to participate in public affairs. In reality, of course, real women and real men lived real lives, and such pretty distinctions between the province of each were frequently violated. The poor and rural of the country, the enslaved, the homeless, the migrants, settlers, vagabonds and thieves, had little time or inclination to consider propriety in manners and comportment, and some of the very wealthy had the option of flouting conventions. Aspiring middle-class women, and some men, sought to spread their values to the shaggy and unwashed hordes through a raft of books advising their readers on the proper bounds of womanhood and the responsibilities of an American mother. Cookbooks, too, did their part in the campaign.

Lydia Maria Child, a truly remarkable writer and reformer, an abolitionist and sometime Swedenborgian, made a specialty of instructing young mothers and poor women in the values and expectations of the aspiring middle class. Not surprisingly, the chowder in her *American Frugal Housewife*, aimed at "those who are not ashamed of economy," shows just a hint of ever-so-restrained refinement:

> *Four pounds of fish are enough to make a chowder for four or five people; half a dozen slices of salt pork in the bottom of the pot; hang it high, so that the pork may not burn; take it out when done very brown; put in a layer of fish, cut in lengthwise slices, then a layer formed of crackers, small or sliced onions, and potatoes sliced as thin as four-pence, mixed with pieces*

of pork you have fried; then a layer of fish again, and so on. Six crackers are enough. Strew a little salt and pepper over each layer; over the whole pour a bowl-full of flour and water, enough to come up even with the surface of what you have in the pot. A sliced lemon adds to the flavor. A cup of tomato catsup is very excellent. Some people put in a cup of beer. A few clams are a pleasant addition. It should be covered so as not to let a particle of steam escape, if possible. Do not open it, except when nearly done, to taste if it be well seasoned

In Child's hands, even catsup, a condiment, showed an awareness of a refined culinary world, with its cloves and allspice, mace, garlic and whole mustard seed. This was not the straightforward fare of ordinary seamen. Other cookbook writers added spices directly into the pot, particularly cloves and mace, and they mixed in herbs such as sweet marjoram, thyme, basil or parsley. Child's contemporary, Catherine Beecher, a reformer from Connecticut and doyenne of proper womanhood, drew from a playbook that echoed elements of both Glasse and Child:

The best fish for chowder haddock and striped bass. Cut the fish in pieces of an inch think, and two inches square. Take six or eight good-size slices of salt pork, and put in the bottom of an iron pot, and fry them in the pot till crisped. Take out the pork, leaving the fat. Chop the pork fine. Put in the pot a layer of fish, a layer of split crackers, some of the chopped pork, black and red pepper, and chopped onions, then another layer of fish, split crackers, and seasoning. This do till you have used your fish. Then just cover the fish with water, and stew slowly till the fish is perfectly tender. Take out the fish, and put it in the dish in which you mean to serve it; set it to keep warm. Thicken the gravy with pounded cracker; add, if you like, mushroom catsup and Port wine. Boil the gravy up once, and pour over the fish; squeeze in the juice of a lemon, and garnish with slices of lemon. If not salt enough from the pork, more must be added.

Fancy catsup, a dash of lemon and a dainty garnish were hardly the only refinements introduced during the early nineteenth century. Cookbook authors improved their chowders by boiling the fish's head, tail and bones to make a stock to use in place of water; they added clam liquor for additional flavor; and they suggested that beer, wine or cider would fortify the dish. A "fine chowder" offered by Eliza Leslie in 1857 was fine, indeed. Identified as a man's recipe—"Commodore Stovens's"—this chowder included fripperies such as mushroom catsup, fresh marjoram and basil, port wine, cloves and mace, and Leslie noted that there were other options for the cook to display her skill: the cod and sea bass that she preferred could be substituted with clams, oysters or crabs, though she insisted on "always beginning the mixture with pork fried with onions." Unlike the rough-and-ready fare of a ship's galley or the beautifully basic food prepared for Ishmael and Queequeg at the Try Pots Inn, the domestic cook was expected to show a wide awareness of the possibilities of food and providing sustenance and to display special skill in its preparation.

In other ways, Child demonstrates that the recipe for chowder was hardly set in stone, and in fact, her recipe hints at what would become three standard elements of the chowder bowl: potato, clams and tomato. A fourth element, dairy, was also wending its way. At some point during the first quarter of the nineteenth century, slices of potato began to insert themselves between the strata of fish and cracker, and within a few short years, the potato more or less supplanted crackers as a thickening agent, often relegating them to little more than a supporting role. Sarah Josepha Hale (author of the immortal "Mary Had a Little

Lamb") might not have been ready to include potatoes in her chowder recipe in 1841, but the "Boston Housekeeper" N.K.M. Lee did in 1832, insisting that her recipe was "according to the most approved method, practiced by fishing parties in Boston harbor." Two decades later, Miss Leslie's Yankee chowder (unlike her "fine chowder") included potatoes side by side with crackers, but two decades further on, Elizabeth Ellet's potato-inclusive recipe let the biscuit merely to reside "on the top of all." For Ellet and others after, the once essential cracker become little more than a garnish, and as Sandra Oliver has noted, by the early twentieth century, crackers were frequently added only at the table, and only by the person eating.

Child's "pleasant addition" of clams points to another innovation in chowder making as the nineteenth century began. Unlike fish, which can be caught from sea or shore, clams were generally collected only from land, typically by digging in mudflats at low tide. Unlike fish, which were hunted primarily by men, in the Native American cultures of New England, clams were gathered primarily by women—although Americans did not make quite the same distinctions. Clams were not a favored food of early colonists—they were fed to swine in normal times and to humans mostly in times of privation—but they gradually came to be accepted, even relished. Today, clam chowder is the default chowder for many, but in Child's time, it was still a novelty, the clams themselves only recently emerging on the plates of the middle and upper classes, acquiring the patina of traditional New England fare. For N.K.M. Lee and others, clam chowder was little more than a fish chowder with potatoes in which the fish was replaced by clams, though it took special effort to separate the hard and leathery parts of the clams from the soft parts. The former were chopped fine (or in some recipes discarded); the latter were added only at the end of the recipe so as not to overcook them. Most clam chowders seem to have included potatoes, and many, like Eliza Leslie's, included spices such as mace or nutmeg. "Let the last layer be clams," Leslie advised, "and then cover the whole with a good paste, and bake it in an iron over, or boil it in an iron pot."

As clams began to dig their way into the chowder bowl, so did dairy, although the latter has never caught the full favor of all chowder cooks. Butter can be found early on mixed with flour to make a thickening agent—Mary Randolph did so in her pioneering cookbook of 1828—but a grander role for dairy was in the offing. In 1845, Esther Howland included both milk and cream in the two chowder recipes she provided (one recipe, lacking pork and onions, was intended for invalids), and from there, the idea seems to have caught on. By 1853, Elizabeth Putnam noted tentatively that "some like half milk and half water" in their chowder, and in 1864, S.G. Knight included "a quart or pint" of milk in her standard recipe, while Thomas De Voe's recipe from 1867 had a two-to-one ratio of water to milk, with a tumbler of claret if one so desired. There were others who objected. Maria Parloa, for one, complained that while some cooks added milk and butter before serving, "for my taste, it is much nicer and more natural without either." Flour could be mixed with butter to "thicken the gravy," as Elizabeth Ellet wrote, or with milk to serve the same purpose.

It seems a shame that such a glorious woman of the Commonwealth as Lydia Maria Child would sully her chowder with tomatoes, but sully she did. If there is a saving grace to her action, it is that her catsup was merely an option, little different than Elizabeth Putnam's suggestion that the fruit could be added "if you like the flavor." For other writers, though, tomatoes soon became a central part of the dish. Although she offered tomato-free recipes for fish chowder (ones that included milk and potato), Juliet Corson packed a whole pint of the red orbs into her clam chowder. In part, we are seeing the beginnings of a regional divergence in chowder that reached its fullest expression in the flowering in the last quarter of the nineteenth century and the establishment of the Boston Cooking School, the most important center of culinary education in New England and the fount for both Mary Lincoln's pioneering *Boston Cook Book* (1884) and Fanny Farmer's enduring *Boston Cooking School Cook Book* (1896).

Mrs. Lincoln offered a stunning array of chowders, including fish, clam, corn and lobster chowder, representing varied techniques and tastes. The last of these, in fact, might not qualify as chowder at all. With boiled milk, lobster and three crackers crushed into fine meal and mixed with butter kneaded with tomalley, it had nary a hint of salt pork. Lincoln's fish chowder was a thing of beauty, bearing all the refinements that women had introduced, from fish stock to potatoes, butter and milk, all meticulously prepared. "Do not soak the crackers in cold water," she warned her readers. "If you wish the broth thicker, stir in one cup of fine cracker crumbs, or one tablespoonful of flour cooked in one tablespoonful of butter. More milk and a little more seasoning may be added to this amount of fish and potato, if you wish a larger quantity." She included options for making a richer soup by beating two eggs into hot milk, making sure not to curdle them, and she suggested that lovers of "highly seasoned food" might enjoy the addition of more onions, cayenne pepper, Worcestershire sauce or curry powder. She advised that many cooks made a superior soup by boiling the haddock with a cod's head, to take advantage of the head's "rich and gelatinous" texture. "In this chowder," she thrilled, "you have nothing but what the most dainty person may relish. There are no bones, skin, or scraps of boiled pork. Fish, potatoes, and crackers are all distinct in the creamy liquid, instead of being a pasty mush, such as is often served. For a change, the crackers may be buttered and browned." This was refinement at its most refined, a showcase for the highest levels of domestic culinary skill.

Landing from the fishing schooner (1905). A postcard showing off a prime location for a turn-of-the-century chowder party. *Courtesy of D.W.*

Fanny Farmer was no less enthused than Mrs. Lincoln, distinguishing several regional variants by name, including Connecticut chowder (the same as fish chowder but with tomatoes in place of milk and with cracker crumbs added just before serving), Rhode Island chowder (including clams, tomatoes and potatoes) and German chowder (with fish dumplings). Since Farmer's time, both Connecticut and Rhode Island have continued down their wayward paths, although Rhode Islanders, at least, have been less consistently perverse. Tomatoes, usually (but not always) with no milk, became characteristic of Connecticut chowders, such as the simple one offered in a 1923 charitable cookbook issued by the Daughters of the American Revolution Chapter in Norwalk, Connecticut:

Three carrots chopped, 3 potatoes chopped; cook in 1½ quarts of water until tender. Grind 2 slices salt pork; fry until brown. Grind 1 large or 3 small onions and brown in pork fat. Add 2 cups tomatoes and cook for 14 minutes. Then add this to

*carrots and potatoes with 2 cups milks and 2 small tablespoons
of flour. Let all boil and season with salt and pepper.*

The recipe was proudly signed by A. Florence Nichols. As for
Rhode Islanders, they have usually held dairy suspect but have
otherwise failed to reach consensus on what should and should
not go into the pot. Potatoes and tomatoes were never considered
by Juliet Corson (though she added a jolt of cider and port), but
Good Housekeeping followed Fanny Farmer in savoring both. The
Ocean State is too small for so many opinions.

Despite all the refinements and elaborations, chowder has
remained a resolutely masculine dish. Corson specifically
indicated that when making chowder "for a party of gentlemen,"
the cook could substitute a half pint of Madeira for the milk,
but such manly touches hardly seemed necessary. Chowder has
retained its status as one of only a handful of distinctly masculine
meals, and while chowder parties often included women as
well as men, its association with the sort of masculine outings
described by William Dyott remained intact, a fitting end to a
day of fishing or sailing. Henry H. Soule (alias Seneca) singled
chowder out as one of the best dishes for "canoe and camp
cookery," and others agreed. Henry David Thoreau enjoyed
a good chowder in the woods after a day of fishing or other
outdoors activity. In one of the more memorable incidents of his
life, he and his friend Edward Hoar accidentally set the woods
aflame near Fair Haven Pond in 1844, when trying to prepare a
fish chowder on a windy day.

The curmudgeonly Harriet Adams put a fine point on
the matter in her 1941 Cape Cod cookbook. "In its day," she
insisted, chowder was the principal part of a meal and "not,
not, one of those fine, thin fugitive soups that you delicately toy
with in a genteel ladies' tea room." Refinement could only do
so much to erase the masculinity of a seafaring dish. The men

of Portsmouth, New Hampshire, certainly thought so when they gathered together in 1873 to celebrate the greatness of their greatest son, Daniel Webster, and noted just how the orator and politician had become a man:

> *Portsmouth stands back upon her chowder; and she not only stands upon her chowder, but she points to what her chowder has done, and says,* "Behold how I take children and make men of them!" *I took Daniel Webster, when he came down from the mountains of New Hampshire…here he was taught how to make a chowder! He took to it kindly. The chowder worked upon that native intellect, which had the capacity to be something in big places, and we sent him forth a giant.* [Emphasis added.]

It is small wonder that chowder appears in *The Stag Cook Book: Written for Men, By Men* (1922), where Walter Louderback proclaims, "The appetite for this dish [the relatively innocuous corn chowder] must be approached from the windy side of promontory in early spring with a sixty pound pack between the shoulder blades." I feel more masculine just reading about it.

Historians sometimes write of manliness and womanliness as gender "roles" being "performed" according to "scripts," but a look at chowder suggests that gender roles are more like jazz improvisation: musical conversations in which the rhythm or melody may be familiar but what a person plays can vary creatively depending on the day and the mood, depending on who accompanies and where and what particular instruments are involved. A woman can transform a masculine dish by bending a few notes, while in the right combo, a man can express his manliness by performing the duties normally assigned to a woman. In the masculine preserve of the firehouse, as Jonathan Deutsch has shown, firemen remain as manly as ever while doing

46

Charlie Delano with a box of clams (circa 1900). *Courtesy of the Local History Room, Kingston Public Library.*

the "woman's work" of cooking or shopping, sometimes by acting more macho than thou to compensate and at other times playing off the femininity of the task. Joking and macho posturing, as much as sincerity, help spackle over the cracks in masculinity.

Aboard ship in the early years of our nation, cooks were often the youngest boys on the crew, and in the nineteenth century, many were of African or Asian descent—all viewed as somehow lesser varieties of men within the dominant culture of the day. In her seminal *Saltwater Foodways*, Sandra Oliver notes that ships' cooks were greeted with an "ambivalent attitude" by their fellow seamen as a result of their unique position aboard ship shuttling between the crewman's forecastle and the officer's quarters. In addition to playing a crucial role in providing the meals, cleaning the galley and washing the pots and pans, cooks could do countless favors for the crew, from drying wet mittens or stockings to fixing treats or slipping special food to the sick or injured. At the mess table, where men ate in a peculiar version of family style, or between watches, joking and macho posturing were as much a part of the culture aboard ship as in the firehouse. Cooks were subjected to a stream of racially or sexually charged jokes and could respond in kind. The bawdiness of sailors is hardly unknown.

Once ashore, chowder's masculine side did not diminish. At shore, as at sea, it was preeminently a social meal, with chowder serving as the centerpiece for chowder parties and clambakes. Chowder masters, usually men, prepared the meal for dozens at a time. Oliver notes how cooks such as Fred Hermes of Mystic, Connecticut, traced their chowder lineage back to earlier masters, connecting to New England's past while performing the important public role of building the reason for the gathering. Chowder master Silas Maxson, Oliver writes, like many others, eschewed exact measurements of ingredients, carefully selecting the right salt pork ("the fat kind, not the streaky kind"), grounding the onions just so, preparing the clams ever so carefully so they would not overcook and cutting his potatoes precisely so that the thin edge of the slice would boil away to act as a thickener. In many ways, chowder masters played the same roles as their wives in the kitchen, or firemen in the firehouse, displaying a rapt attention to the techniques of cooking and selection of ingredients and lavishing their community of sharers with an intense and bonding care.

Right: Advertisement for Philips Delicious Clam Chowder Condensed. *Courtesy of the New England Chowder Compendium.*

Below: A pot of chowder at dusk by mud flats.

A quahog, also known as a chowder clam.

A fresh chowder with oyster crackers.

Chowder crackers: (clockwise from left) butter, common, oyster and pilot.

Common chowder foundations: salt pork and bacon.

Three vegetables for chowder.

A bowl of cod chowder with common crackers and pieces of salt pork.

Littlenecks and a rake.

Right: Razor clams and mussels.

Below: An oyster.

Salt pork in three stages: uncooked, cooking and cracklings.

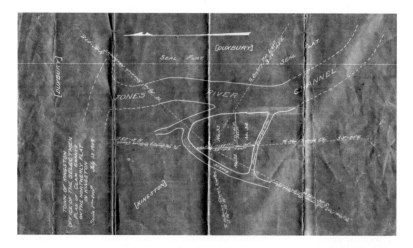

Plan of a clam grant for the North East flat in Kingston, Massachusetts. *Courtesy of the Local History Room, Kingston Public Library.*

A pot of chowder by the bay.

A warm cup of chowder on a wooden table.

Seven ingredients for chowder.

The Anatomy of Chowder

Invasion, theft, murder and wanton devastation are not the first things that occur to a person when tucking into a bowl of delicious chowder, but deep in its very making, ingrained ingredient by ingredient, chowder bears the traces of a violent past. This most comfortable of comfort foods carries a subtle aftertaste of international conflict, of conquest and enslavement, of the blood and tears that made Europe imperial and shaped the modern world. Every bowl is a reminder of those earlier phases of globalization when the rise of a new ideology of empire was animated by the even newer ideology of capitalism, unleashing swarms of ships into the farthest seas to vie violently for the chance to subjugate the "lesser" peoples of the globe and capture their natural riches for the imperial powers of Europe. In fishing scows and merchants' sloops, no less than in heavily armed ships of war, the contest was fought hot and cold on every wave, with every port an opportunity for advantage.

Every bowl of chowder contains the soup of colonial desire and the scent of a painful past. Every dish is a cauldron of remembrance and forgetting. To anatomize a bowl of chowder, to tease apart its handful of ingredients, is to read the history of British North America in miniature; it is to understand how deeply the wars of empire ran and how empire influenced our everyday lives in ways too numerous to count, too subtle to notice. To follow just four ingredients—salt pork, potatoes, fish and clams—is to follow how our nation has come to be.

SALT PORK

Neither native intelligence nor animal charm, or even the unfortunate tendency toward deliciousness, has served the pig particularly well. Pigs have bad press. George Orwell painted a grim portrait of swine as fascist autocrats, the Book of Leviticus condemns them as unclean and it seems that every goodhearted Wilbur in *Charlotte's Web* is matched by a pitiful Piggy in *Lord of the Flies*. Whether it is psychological compensation among those who cannot contemplate eating sentient beings or the consequence of being an animal whose odor too often precedes it, pigs have suffered just for being pigs, becoming symbols of gluttony and greed, sloth and self-interest, filth and squalor.

As unfair as this reputation may be, there may actually be reasons why our pleasant porkers have become so despised, and as much as we hate to admit it, Orwell's vision of bullies subjugating their fellow animals may not be so far from the mark. Buried deep in the mists of American memory is the uncomfortable fact that pigs once served as the shock troops of invasion. Almost from the moment of their arrival in the New World, they became an essential element of European survival, not just as reliable sources of food but also as fellow conquerors. They became the flashpoint for conflict between colonists and the indigenous population, a hammer to the environmental nail and a ready excuse for violence on any occasion.

Although the New World was home to two species of pigs prior to the arrival of Europeans, domestic pigs (*Sus scrofa*) were absent. Having savored the suckling since before the dawn of written history, the Spanish could not imagine leaving their bacon behind as they extended their imperial hand across the Atlantic. Colonizing first the Canary Islands and then the Azores, Madeira and Cape Verde, pigs leapt to the Caribbean with Columbus himself, landing on the island of Española in 1493. Easy to transport by ship and just as easy to drive once ashore, pigs were an almost ideal food for the invaders. Most of a pig's body weight is converted efficiently into edible pork or lard, and even more importantly in the New World, they are hardy, adaptable, omnivorous and, above all, prolific. They were, as the historian R.A. Donkin has noted, "admirably suited to an age of exploration and colonization," reflecting many of the pioneer qualities of the conquistadores they accompanied—including (as Donkin demurs from mentioning) a certain rapacity.

In the New World, pigs were fruitful, indeed, and multiplied. From José de Acosta to José Fernández de Oviedo, chroniclers of the Spanish conquest noted how wonderfully pigs thrived in the new colonies. Within a scant dozen years of their arrival, the hogs from Española seeded new populations of swine in Puerto Rico (1505–08), Jamaica (1509), Cuba (1511), Colombia (1516?), Panama (1519) and Peru (1540), accompanying the conquistadors as they slashed their way through native empires and verdant lands. As Cortes invaded Honduras in 1526–27, his troops marched step by step with *una gran manada de puercos* (a large herd of swine), and when Hernando de Soto probed Florida in about 1540, a formidable column of pigs explored with him, side by side. Everywhere they went, their numbers swelled. By 1700, thirty thousand pigs were consumed annually in Mexico City alone, and in remote areas, on islands and on desolate shores, Spanish and Portuguese explorers set pigs loose to do their piggy best at breeding, expecting that future survivors of shipwrecks or settlers would one day be able to reap the benefits of a healthy piggery. The descendants of pigs left on Ossabaw Island, Georgia, still run today, little changed by the years. Closer to the home of chowder, the English writer Humphrey Gilbert (1583) asserted that it was the Portuguese who introduced swine to Nova Scotia, laying the base for years of future chowder.

Not to be outdone by their Spanish rivals, the English also imported pigs to their North American colonies, and swine became familiar characters in the early years of Massachusetts Bay, Plymouth and Rhode Island. As historians Virginia DeJohn Anderson and Peter Karsten have shown, pigs in New England might be seen as agents provocateurs as much as candidates for a barbecue. For hundreds of years, English farmers had successfully raised livestock on small plots of land, using fencing to maintain proper relations with neighbors. So successful were they, in fact, that the law governing animal husbandry had evolved to suit the conditions in the fields. In the Middle Ages, the onus of fence building fell on cultivators, who were held responsible for fencing animals out of anywhere mischief could be done, but by 1600, the legal burden had shifted to livestock owners, who were held responsible for not fencing their animals. Yet when New England was settled, the economics of livestock production in this new and unenclosed land led Puritan authorities to return to the older practice, requiring cultivators to fence livestock out. To begin with, livestock were too important to the new economy to limit them, but more than that, the availability of "unimproved" land was too tempting to pass up. Throughout the British North American colonies, husbandmen found it more economical to set their hyper-reproductive pigs loose to forage in the forests rather than keep them penned up and close at hand. With little investment, a little luck and almost no financial input from the farmer, a herd would find its own food, sustain itself and increase. There truly were profits in the wilderness.

This new form of low-investment husbandry, however, came with hidden costs. Swine are not known for their restraint, and with literally no boundaries to restrain them, they roamed wherever they wished, into neighbors' fields and beyond into the surrounding woods and pastures. Pigs, to say the least, respected no one. Technically, New England husbandmen were required by law to yoke their pigs or ring them through the nose, and stray animals could be shot if they got into mischief in a neighbor's holdings, but strays were nevertheless numerous, and in a land where colonists were as quick to sue as their swine were quick to gobble a neighbor's corn, the courts were kept busy.

Wounds from such conflicts ran raw. In 1692, for example, Sarah Holton's pigs were found in her neighbor Rebecca Nurse's fields in Salem Village, gorging themselves on her corn. Holton insisted that her swine had been "sufficiently yoaked" and that the fences were down "in severall places," implying that Nurse was at fault for the transgression, but Nurse would have none of it. Refusing to be pacified, she commenced "railing and scolding agrat while," finally calling her son to "git a gun and kill [Holton's] piggs and lett non of them goe out of the field." Although no pigs died that day, neither did the conflict. A short time later, Sarah's husband, Benjamin, was stricken with a "strainge fitt," followed by blindness and "a cruel death." Suspicions immediately fell on Nurse, and Sarah Holton joined a chorus of other aggrieved neighbors in accusing Nurse of malevolent witchcraft. Nurse met her end on the Salem gallows on July 19, 1692, one of nineteen to die in the witch hysteria.

It would be hard to understate how much more volatile such cases became when the aggrieved parties were not fellow Englishmen but Indians. Accusations of witchcraft and murder were comparatively minor affairs, but warfare, formal and informal, was a constant threat. Recognizing the incendiary potential of marauding swine, the authorities in Massachusetts

Bay passed a law in 1640 requiring settlers either to restrain their livestock or to assist in building fences that the Indians were required to maintain. In theory, Indians had access to colonial courts to air their grievances, and in practice, they exercised those rights, occasionally even winning judgments against their offending Puritan neighbors. Yet in practice, the results could be more frustrating than the incidents that sparked them. As if the story were written by Franz Kafka (if Kafka had cared about pigs), Indians were allowed to sue, but only in a court that ran on unfamiliar legal principles, that operated in a foreign tongue and that required the plaintiff to demonstrate after the fact that he had maintained his fences in good order. Regardless of the outcome, the authorities had only limited ability to enforce the law locally, and a favorable verdict meant little when an armed mob of angry Englishmen appeared at the edge of one's field. Even if a farmer could keep his fields livestock free, livestock could graze freely and legally on any "waste" land (land not "improved" by fencing, clearing or pasturing). Nearly the entirety of Indian hunting grounds was therefore fair game, so to speak, and since English settlers could legally claim property rights over land they had improved themselves, there was actually incentive to set the pigs loose. A grazing pig was a claim to ownership over the land they grazed.

As if this situation were not dire enough, when pigs roamed into the hunting grounds, they were vulnerable to Indian deer traps, leading to a raft of lawsuits from colonists demanding compensation for their lost livestock. The point of this roaming, of course, was to forage for food, and if pigs excel at anything as much as breeding, it is foraging. The ever-resourceful swine soon learned to pry into the Indians' underground storage pits, to root up clams that Indian women collected at low tide and to steal other foods, all while unintentionally chasing game animals away. Pigs also exacerbated the environmental changes set in motion by English settlers. While New England Indians had altered the land in many ways before the arrival of Europeans, the influx of British settlers left far more profound scars. After clearing fields; draining wetlands; damming and rerouting streams; fencing plots; disrupting the native ecology; introducing new diseases, plants and animals; and overhunting the native fish, fowl and fur bearers, the pigs swept in. Rooting through forest floors, pigs swept up the Indian staples of acorns and nuts; they gobbled berries and roots and tore up the tender shoots of plants, depriving other animals of food in the process. As efficient as they are at eating, pigs set off a chain reaction of environmental degradation that ended always in loss and privation for native peoples.

The Wampanoag, Massachusett and other tribes were not passive when confronting this calamity, nor did they rely simply on the courts. They adapted. Raising livestock required significant adjustments from New England Indians, requiring new ways of thinking about animals, nature and spirituality; new ways of thinking about labor; new ways of thinking about food and subsistence; and new ways of approaching men's work and women's work. But adjust they did. While many Indian villages resisted the adoption of livestock, others, particularly those that had converted to Christianity, saw virtues in swine. To English eyes, native agricultural practices had never risen to the level of improvement and therefore, according to English law, Indians had never secured rights to the lands they occupied. As the English saw it (in part erroneously), the Indians built no fences and had no private property, no sedentary agriculture and no livestock to speak of. Only by becoming "civilized," by adopting English patterns of life, could they claim a rightful place in the new New England.

Some Indians did seek that rightful place, and swine were among their preferred avenues to "civilization." English missionaries like John Eliot and Jonathan Mayhew introduced pigs and cattle to Christian converts in the "praying towns" of Natick, Hassanamessit and Punkapaog, on Cape Cod, Martha's Vineyard and Nantucket, respectively, and under intense pressure from English encroachment on their lands, many Indians recognized that grazing a few animals gave them rights to the land under English law, while for converts, the herds also served as a concrete symbol of their new commitment to Christianity. The historian David Silverman has shown how the Wampanoags and other tribes—Christian and non-Christian—adapted animal raising to match their own cultural beliefs, gaining a measure of protection from the encroaching English, but this apparent path to security was a hard one. Maintaining herds and entering fully into the English economy left them vulnerable to the fate that befalls all debtors, and particularly after the Wampanoags began undercutting English prices when selling pork to Boston, the colonial authorities began to intervene.

Facing such bitter circumstances, some Indians took matters into their own hands, retaliating against stray pigs and cattle, not only deepening the enmity with the colonists but also exposing the killer to prosecution in English courts. As English herds swelled—in large part because of their use of Indian lands—the English demand for land swelled correspondingly, ratcheting up tensions further. Retribution, self-protection, interference and nullification in court produced a situation that nearly erupted in war in 1671, when a group of colonists near Natick threatened the Wampanoags of nearby Mount Hope for killing swine. When full-fledged war came four years later—King Philip's War—the region from the Berkshires to the bay ignited in flame, with herds of swine and cattle taking the brunt of Indian attacks, both to deprive the colonists of food and to make off with supplies they could use later. Not surprisingly, cattle and pigs became symbols of the conflict between Indian and white and became the special targets of Indian reprisal. After initial successes, the Indians

A bowl of clam chowder with kernels of corn and chunks of fried salt pork.

were crushed, and thousands were killed. Indian resistance in New England was virtually annihilated.

The sad history of New England swine is little more than a backdrop to the story of salt pork, the base ingredient in chowder, but the story sets the stage for the years that followed. Fresh pork was certainly consumed in early New England, but with such a perishable product, some method of preserving the meat for the longer term was essential. Although dry salting, brining and smoking were all practiced, brining was the most popular method in early New England to keep pork. After boiling in salt-saturated water and being allowed to cool, the pork was packed tightly in a barrel under a heavy weight, and as Lydia Maria Child assured, meat packed this way would "continue good twenty years." Recipes for salt pork can be found in most early cookbooks, and salt pork was consumed year-round. The pork barrel was a ubiquitous feature of New England farmsteads, but because it preserved so well, it became a key part of the rations that fed colonial armies and navies as they went about their business of protecting and extending the empire. Barrels of salt pork could easily be transported as New Englanders spread westward to settle new lands in New York and the Midwest, new lands appropriated from the native population, and barrels could be shipped anywhere New Englanders sailed, to feed the crews who spread American economic and (later) military power abroad.

Even in death, the pig was the expansionist's best friend.

POTATOES

If taste were eternal, Martha Stewart might be queen, but alas it is not and she is not. Taste and tastes respond to the ebb and flow of supply and demand, and just as surely they adapt to new foods and new methods of preparation. There was a time when our New England forebears considered Maine lobsters, so beloved of today's gourmets, to be mere "garbage fish," fit only for swine or famine times, and the starchy potato, now so well loved, went through odd travels from being a luxury item for the elite to rejection by the poor to becoming the staple of much of the North Atlantic world. Humble and homely, yet satisfying, the potato is a relative newcomer to the chowder bowl, taking nearly half a century to slide its way between the strata of fish and cracker, but ever since it first dove between, the potato has played a crucial supporting role as thickener, flavor base and heft.

Americans today consume nearly four hundred pounds of potatoes annually, and while new varieties find their way to the market regularly—boilers, bakers or fryers in a bruised rainbow of colors—they all share an enormously long history. Cultivated in the Andean highlands of South America for millennia, the potato was so important to the native cultures there that the Ancient Incas were said to have measured time by how long potatoes took to cook. The Spanish conquistadors certainly noticed these valuable commodities, and many of the great names in the early history of Spanish and English imperial expansion are tied up in tuberous history. In 1536, less than a decade after the fall of the Inca Empire, Conquistador Juan de Castellanos became the first European to mention potatoes, writing that they were "a gift very acceptable to the Indian, and a dainty dish even for the Spaniard." Castellanos's esteem, however, was not universally shared, even though several of his fellow conquerors remarked that the tuber was central to the civilizations they were laying to waste. Gold and silver were simply more alluring. Within a few decades, however, the fortunes of the potato began to wax, and this exotic but ugly tuber with the long shelf life would be adopted widely as a cheap food for slaves and a nutritious commodity to stock ships' larders.

Potatoes arrived in Europe to much less fanfare than the galleons of precious metals stripped from Inca coffers, but they nevertheless left a mark on the written record. Redcliffe Salaman, perhaps the most enthusiastic of tuber historians, discovered that in the fall of 1576, potatoes appeared as a line item in the account books of the Hospital de la Sangre in Seville, the seat of Spanish colonial administration, the first record of a continental spud. Potatoes had arrived in Europe, and from this inauspicious day forward, they flowered. By 1584, Salaman notes, the quantities ordered by the hospital rose from just a few pounds at a time to tens of pounds. In the span of a few brief years, the potato had gone from being a specialty crop purchased in small quantities to a staple raised on a commercial scale. Because tubers could not remain viable for long once uprooted, Salaman theorized that potatoes must have traveled the migratory route of pigs in reverse: hopping from island settlement to island settlement. At each stop, they were cultivated until the quantity was sufficient to make the next step forward. Sure enough, John Reader, a worthy successor to Salaman, reports finding a record of potatoes in the Canary Islands in 1567, halfway across the Atlantic, at which time, he notes, a barrel of tubers was sent to Antwerp. Whether these potatoes were ever planted or just consumed, it appears that the Belgian love affair with pommes frites had an early start.

By the third quarter of this century of European imperial expansion, the potato was being raised and consumed widely in continental Europe. In 1588, the Flemish horticulturist Carolus Clusius (the man who introduced the tulip to the Netherlands) saw potatoes growing in Italian gardens, and at more or less the same time, the English showed that they could be as hot on Spanish heels in raising tubers as they were in raising an empire. In fact, the history of the potato in England begins on heels made hot from piracy. During the reign of Queen Elizabeth I, the story goes, an English ship transporting slaves to the Spanish Main was attacked at the port of San Juan de Ulua and burned. A young sailor from County Devon aboard that ship, Francis Drake, barely managed to escape with his life, never forgetting or forgiving, the bitter experience transforming him into an avenging angel for the British Crown.

From that point on, Drake spent his career wreaking havoc on the Spanish fleet as a pirate for hire, often under the cloak of high secrecy. In 1577, he led a flotilla of five ships along the African coast and from thence into the Pacific, then dominated by Spain, and for the next two years, he harassed Spanish shipping from Chile to California (where he was the first Englishman to land), puncturing their sense of invulnerability while racking up the ultimate prize: a fully laden Spanish treasure ship. Returning to England to

Sitting flush with the deck, a prism could illuminate the underbelly of a ship with natural light from above.

earn a knighthood for his depredations, Drake returned to the Caribbean conflict in 1586 to sack Santo Domingo, Cartagena and St. Augustine, and two years later still, he helped send the Spanish Armada to the bottom of the English Channel.

In the midst of this rampage, Drake may have helped introduce the potato to England. Although the event is unrecorded, it seems possible that Drake became acquainted with the potato during his devastation of the Pacific (which, after all, paralleled the heartland of the tuber), and there is evidence that he and others soon grasped the food's value for ships' stores. Off the coast of Chile in November 1578, Drake reported that people flocked to his ships to offer potatoes and fat sheep, and off Concepción, Chile, in 1587, Master Perry, accompanying the expedition of Thomas Cavendish, similarly wrote of receiving "cases of straw filled with potato rootes, which were very good to eat, ready made up in the store houses for the Spanish against they should come for this tribute." Kept relatively dry, the potato lasted well aboard ship and provided a nutritious, versatile and satisfying meal for the crew. In other words, the potato planted itself in ships' larders.

Precisely when the potato arrived in England is a bit less clear. The careful botanist Clusius failed to notice potatoes when he visited Drake in England in 1581, suggesting that our piratical Prometheus did not bring them directly home from the Pacific (assuming even that they could survive). The decade, however, was a crucial one for English attempts at building an Atlantic empire, and there were other opportunities for the potato to make its way to the green and pleasant land. In 1585, Thomas Harriot accompanied Richard Grenville on the second English expedition to Virginia, a voyage financed by the queen's favorite, Sir Walter Raleigh, and after a year at Roanoke Island, he and most of his party were whisked back home by Drake, just returning from his sack of Cartagena. The 107,000 ducats Drake had won for ransoming the city may have been accompanied by an even more valuable prize: the potato. Raleigh himself, Salaman speculates, may have introduced the potato into Ireland in 1586 or 1588.

It was not long before proper descriptions of the potato began to appear in print. "Herbals," compendia of botanical knowledge intended for use in medical applications, as well as gardening and farming, were an ancient genre of book and wildly popular. The first published notice of the potato came from the English botanical pirate, John Gerard, who reported growing the potato in his garden in Holborn in 1596. One year later, in

December 1597, he described the potato at length in his *Herbal*, which became one of the most widely read English herbals of the century. "It groweth naturally in America," Gerard wrote, "where it was first discovered as reports C. Clusius, since which time I have received roots thereof from Virginia, otherwise called Norumbega, which grow and prosper in my garden as in their native country." Before the first permanent English settlement in North America, before Jamestown, the potato was counted as a fruit of new world conquest. To illustrate this exotic new plant, Gerard liberated woodcuts made ten years before by Jacob Bergzaben (also known as Tabernaemontanus) for his *Neuw Kreuterbuch* (1588).

Gerard's description of the "Potatoes of Virginia" did not help establish the plant on a sound botanical footing. "This plant (which is called by some *Sisarum Peruvianum*, or Scyrrets of Peru), is generally of us called Potatus or Potatoes," he wrote accurately enough, but there is some confusion over whether Gerard distinguished the common potato (*Solanum tuberosa*) that Drake might have obtained from Cartagena from the three edible tubers that Harriot reported being used by the Virginia Indians, one of which was called the Indian potato or bog potato (*Apios tuberosa*). Salaman speculates that Gerard may have grown both the Indian potato and the bog potato in his garden, with his apparent confusion between the two arising from political motives—his desire to ingratiate himself with Queen Elizabeth by displaying the first fruits of the new colony she placed under the aegis of her favorite, Walter Raleigh. Intentionally or not, this was an interesting case of the English colonizers thieving credit for the thievery of Spanish imperialists, and the false Virginia connection was propagated by writers for decades to follow.

From the time of Shakespeare through the English Civil Wars of the 1640s and '50s, the potato gained a decidedly mixed reputation. Both Salaman and Reader note that Clusius and the botanist

Gaspard Bauhin believed the potato to be good primarily for producing flatulence and "for exciting Venus"—two concepts not normally conjoined—or in the inimitable words of the horticulturist John Goodyer (1637), potatoes "comfort, nourish and strengthen the body procuring bodily lust and that with greediness." Yes, the reputation of the potato as a flatulent aphrodisiac overshadowed its nutritive value, and they were still a relatively costly luxury food when John Forster and other writers began turning that reputation around by touting them as a food for the masses.

Following more than twenty years of Civil War, the beheading of one king and the return of another, Forster believed that the potato could solve the problem of hunger among the uprooted masses of peasants. Since they could be grown nearly anywhere, in poor soils and dubious climate, and because they stored well, potatoes could be a safeguard against famine. The poor, however, too often failed to see the logic. While the Irish and the northern counties of England adopted the potato avidly, in southern England and most of western Europe, small cottagers, peasants and the poor resisted the best intentions of well-to-do do-gooders like Forster. Unlike the grains that had traditionally formed the basis of peasant diets, potatoes were typically by tubers rather than seed, requiring farmers already living on the edge of failure to make a risky adjustment in their practices, and every acre set in potatoes displaced an acre of more familiar food. Folktales about the ill effects of the potato added to a dire reputation. In France, they were said to have been banned for causing leprosy, while they were associated with scrofula, rickets or consumption in Germany. In Scotland and Russia, they were rejected because they were not mentioned in the Bible and therefore thought not designed for humanity.

By the late eighteenth century, however, resistance to the potato among the poor began to fade. According to the historian John Reader, the ravages of invading armies in the ceaseless imperial warfare left the potato as one of the few reliable food sources. Even after crops were trampled and plundered by armies, peasants could return to their fields to dig up their tubers and survive. Soldiers would take any stores they could find and burn the rest, but they seldom made the extra effort to root in the ground (perhaps they should have brought more pigs). Fortuitously for the peasantry of Europe, potatoes provide four times more calories for the same amount of land as grain, so that even after the armies left, the greater efficiency of the plant led to better economic results. Wherever wars afflicted Europe, potatoes followed, becoming part of an evolving diet, and when peace reigned, the better nutrition potatoes afforded helped swell the population, leaving an expanding demographic base that fed the dark Satanic mills of the early industrial revolution. The potato "came as a heaven-sent gift to the leaders of industry," according to Salaman. "Its use was urged not only by the employers, but by many well-intentioned persons who failed to appreciate its implications." Cheap and plentiful food enabled industrialists to keep wages low.

According to Salaman, the potato was brought to America (or back to America) by "a group of Irish Presbyterians" in 1719, and by the end of the century, it had attained a place at the hearth here, too, though only slowly. Although John Thorne remarks that potatoes apparently did not enter the Cape Cod diet significantly until the mid-nineteenth century, they were eagerly sought elsewhere. In 1796, Amelia Simmons, author of the first cookbook written by an American for Americans, remarked that "a good potato comes up in many branches of cookery" and takes "rank for universal use, profit and easy acquirement." Already familiar with several varieties of potato available in New England, each with its own distinctive qualities, Simmons noted that they could be roasted or boiled and used for stuffing or pies or in a potato pudding or potato cake. Nevertheless, the potato still seemed to bear the stamp of an import in the United States.

In discussing how to raise them, she wrote, "All potatoes run out, or depreciate in America; a fresh importation of the Spanish might restore them to table use."

It was not long before they were thoroughly adopted. By the time of the Civil War, Catherine Beecher and Harriet Beecher Stowe considered their "staunch old friend" to be the staff of life: "Like bread, it is held as a sort of sine-qua-non; like that, it may be made invariably palatable by a little care in a few plain particulars." Like the industrial revolution, the potato had become essential.

FISH

Hanging high above the chamber of the Massachusetts House of Representatives is a four-foot, eleven-inch pine carving of a cod, the Sacred Cod of Massachusetts. Grand, painted and fully life size, this particular cod was a gift to the commonwealth in 1784 from John Rowe, the merchant (smuggler, to be more accurate) and politician whose cargo was dumped overboard during the Boston Tea Party, but it is actually the third in a distinguished line of cods. The first, rumored to have been presented by Samuel Sewall, a judge at the Salem witch trials, went up in flames in 1747, along with the entire statehouse. Its replacement survived a Patriot mob during the American Revolution but went missing when the British occupied the city, leaving the current one as the longest lived and most experienced cod in history. Sacred and otherwise, the cod has enjoyed a uniquely privileged view of the history of the commonwealth, our politics and economy, and in its mute and wooden way, it represents some of the complex meanings the cod has had in New England culture.

Symbolically, the cod has reigned over New England from a watery throne from the beginning of European settlement; it has been a commodity, a spur to trade, a torch to the fuel of imperial

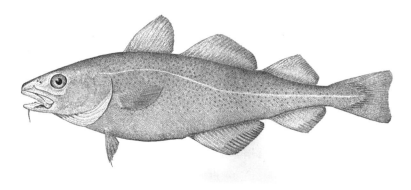

Etching of a codfish. *United States Commission of Fish and Fisheries (1897).*

conflict and sustenance for the masses throughout the hemisphere. Within four years of the arrival of the Puritans at Plymouth Rock, fifty British ships could be found plying the waters off Cape Cod, harvesting fish, and by 1640, Massachusetts fisherman had brought 300,000 cod to market. The lucrative trade in fish filled the coffers of the colony's "codfish aristocracy," building fortunes unimaginable to the earliest settlers and political power to match. Going to sea became a rite of passage for working-class men in much of New England, a stage of life for nearly all and a life's career for many. From Portland to Provincetown, dozens of communities were entirely dependent on the industry, with some, like Gloucester, mooring hundreds of ships. So important was the cod to the commonwealth that when the new Massachusetts statehouse was dedicated in January 1798, the third Sacred Cod was deposed from its perch in the old building, solemnly marched to the new one wrapped in an American flag and carefully resuspended. It would not be a mistake to say that New England was founded by an act of cod or that cod and nation were one. Our familiar grade-school narrative would have us believe that the Puritans came to our shores to establish the rule of God, but it was the lure of cod instead that attracted the first Englishmen.

For generations, the European demand for cod had been filled by the active fisheries of Iceland, but the discovery of the astonishingly prolific fishing grounds that stretched from Labrador and Newfoundland to Massachusetts transformed the geography of the North Atlantic. The prize, it seemed, was an inexhaustible store of ground fish, already a dietary staple in much of Europe. The vast and teeming shoals of fish left witnesses incredulous. After hearing from the explorer John Cabot about the waters off Newfoundland in December 1497, Raimondo di Soncino wrote to the Duke of Milan that "the sea there is swarming with fish, which can be taken not only with a net but in baskets let down with a stone." Perhaps cod did not actually leap into the boat and gut themselves, but Cabot's son, Sebastian, remarked that they were so plentiful in places that ships could barely pass. This was a bonanza, an endless supply of protein. "It is the land of the cod fish!" wrote the Abbé Ferland, as translated by the cod historian Harold Innis. "Your eyes and nose, your tongue and throat and ears as well, soon make you realize that in the peninsula of Gaspé the codfish forms the basis alike of food and amusements, of business and general talk, of regrets, hope, good luck, everyday life—I would almost be ready to say of existence itself." Already bred into our culture, Soncino was convinced that the cod offered nothing less than strategic independence from foreign powers. The fishing fleet "could bring so many fish," he wrote, "that this Kingdom would have no further need of Iceland."

By 1502, the Portuguese were already prowling the cod lands, with the Spanish close behind, and the two empires were soon afflicted with Basque, English, Bretons, Normans and Dutch. Barely a decade after Columbus's arrival in the New World, the rising empires of Europe all vied for prime spots on the barren northern shores, planting settlements only to service their fleets during their long seasonal voyages.

A half step behind their rivals, the English were propelled into the competition by the failure of the Icelandic fisheries at mid-century and by a steadily rising demand at home. To encourage the English industry, Edward VI proclaimed "political Lent" during his brief reign in 1548, requiring his subjects to eat fish on Fridays, Ember Days and during Lent itself. Adding to the incentive, the Crown enacted tax holidays between 1564 and 1574, and thereafter it relied on a nearly steady state of warfare and piracy to settle the matter of control over the fishing grounds. After the destruction of the Spanish Armada in 1588 finally broke the Iberian grip, the English and French were the only ones left standing to dominate the region, and rights to the fishery became a perpetually unhealed sore through conflicts from Queen Anne's War to the American Revolution.

War was not the only challenge. Finding a way to preserve the fish properly was essential in the days before refrigeration, and with the technology of the day, the best way to preserve cod for the long voyage that lay ahead was salting or brining. Split, packed in salt and laid out to dry, the cod became as stiff as a board, and about as durable, ready to ship anywhere a ship could travel for as long as it would take to get there. Blessed with a climate that ensured an abundant supply of salt through the evaporation of seawater, the Mediterranean countries held an early edge, even after figuring in the cost of transporting a bulky, low-value product like salt. The English had no such steady supply. As a consequence, they focused their efforts on a relatively lightly salted product made by laying fish out on shore to dry in the sun and wind. Where the French salted their catch in the holds of their ships, preserving them on the go, the English were spurred to claim broad stretches of land for their drying operations, and from these footholds eventually sprang more permanent settlements. When Bartholomew Gosnold sailed down from Nova Scotia in search of sassafras in 1602, he stumbled upon what would become one of the best of these permanent settlements, a place he called Cape Cod in honor of the fish that "pestered" him there. The rich marine fauna and the presence of a rocky, wind-swept shore made the Cape a perfect base for the cod fishery, and where earlier fishing had been strictly seasonal, ships returning home between voyages, the calendar now lay unconstrained.

So the cycle began. By the early 1600s, the fishing fleets from both the West Country of England and New England began to swell, and the settlements on shore grew ever more solid. The demand for cod rose steadily, too, driven in part by the needs of an army and navy locked in combat with their imperial rivals, and with the attempt to subjugate the wild Irish, and in part by a steady rise in population at home. War was as good for business as breeding. Salt cod was a particularly desirable commodity for trade with the Catholic countries of Europe, where *bacalao* (*bacalhau* in Portuguese) is still an integral part of the cuisine. In its back-and-forth way, cod drove demand for imports on the western side of the Atlantic, both to supply settlers and the shipping fleet and to meet the rising demand for luxury goods among prosperous seafarers. If pigs set off a chain reaction of environmental degradation in New England, cod set off a chain reaction of consumption.

The degree to which New England towns were dedicated to the fish and fishery cannot be understated. In some towns, nearly every-able bodied male spent time fishing, and ashore, the industry left its mark wherever one looked. This was visibly the land of the codfish. With tongue ever so slightly in cheek, Henry David Thoreau described Provincetown in a way that reveals how much salt fish had entered the veins of the New England economy:

> *A great many of the houses here were surrounded by fish-flakes*
> *close up to the sills on all sides, with only a narrow passage two*

70

or three feet wide, to the front door; so that instead of looking out into a flower or grass plot, you looked on to so many square rods of cod turned wrong side outwards. These parterres were said to be least like a flower-garden in a good drying day in mid-summer. There were flakes of every age and pattern, and some so rusty and overgrown with lichens that they looked as if they might have served the founders of the fishery here. Some had broken down under the weight of successive harvests. The principal employment of the inhabitants at this time seemed to be to trundle out their fish and spread them in the morning, and bring them in at night. I saw how many a loafer who chanced to be out early enough got a job at wheeling out the fish of his neighbor who was anxious to improve the whole of a fair day. Now, then, I knew where salt fish were caught. They were everywhere lying on their backs, their collar-bones standing out like the lapels of a man-o'-war-man's jacket, and inviting all things to come and rest in their bosoms; and all things, with a few exceptions, accepted the invitation. I think, by the way, that if you should wrap a large salt fish round a small boy, he would have a coat of such a fashion as I have seen many a one wear to muster. Salt fish were stacked up on the wharves, looking like corded wood, maple and yellow birch with the bark left on. I mistook them for this at first, and such in one sense they were—fuel to maintain our vital fires—an eastern wood which grew on the Grand Banks. Some were stacked in the form of huge flower-pots, being laid in small circles with the tails outwards, each circle successively larger than the preceding until the pile was three or four feet high, when the circles rapidly diminished, so as to form a conical roof.

A remarkable food, cod was cheap to produce and boasted a protein content that approached 80 percent when dried. Nearly every part of the fish could be used, from the tongue and head to the sound (aid bladder), the roe and the vitamin-rich liver. But not all cod was the same. The highest-quality fish were sent to the cod-ravenous cooks of Catholic Europe, where by the middle of the seventeenth century nearly 60 percent of the fish eaten was salt cod, and other high-quality fish went to England. The inferior product—the refuse fish—was not a total waste, however, finding their market in the West Indian plantations and (later) the American South to feed a burgeoning enslaved population. Almost half the salt cod produced in 1750 was sent to the sugar fields of the Caribbean, forming an integral link in the famous triangular trade. In its fullest expression, the triangular trade linked Europe, Africa and the American colonies in a single extended economy supporting and supported by slavery. Unloading their cod or timber in Europe, New England ships transported manufactured goods or African slaves to the West Indies, and from there, they loaded up with back sugar and molasses to be distilled into rum at home. Salt cod, in other words, sustained slavery as much as it sustained the slaves themselves.

With profits to be made in almost any port from imperial adventures, the tastes of Catholics and the scarred backs of slaves, New England merchants became notoriously aggressive in their trading, and with so much money at stake, the ugly specter of competition flared. At the Treaties of Utrecht in 1713 and Paris in 1763, the French and English ended wars but were unable to end their conflict over the great fishing banks. Even within the British Empire itself, conflict over cod and commerce was rife. As Parliament grasped for ways to regulate commerce to imperial advantage, colonial merchants went about their business, licit and illicit. Beginning in 1651, Parliament passed a series of Trade and Navigation Acts aimed at ensnaring all colonial trade within imperial markets, first attempting to prohibit non-English ships from trading in colonial ports and then constraining the trade in certain goods, such as molasses and sugar, to English ports. Although enforcement was lax and did little to impede the illicit trade, the Crown made few friends in New England. The historian Christopher Magra has suggested that while salt cod was not specifically targeted, the competition between New Englanders, West Country fishing interests and West Indian planters set an important backdrop for the Trade and Navigation Acts.

It is hardly coincidental that in 1775, as revolution became reality, Parliament prohibited colonial vessels from fishing the banks of Newfoundland, the Gulf of St. Lawrence and the coasts of Labrador and Nova Scotia, nor is it coincidence that during the peace negotiations that ended the American Revolution—as at the end of every imperial war—fishing rights became one of the most contentious issues to resolve. Although guaranteed the right to continue fishing the Grand Banks and Canadian shores at the Treaty of Paris in 1783, American vessels were denied access to their drying stations in Newfoundland. As with every previous imperial conflict, the Peace of Paris failed to settle the

Stripping a cod. *United States Commission of Fish and Fisheries (1897).*

matter, and for thirty years, the new United States and Great Britain contended with tit-for-tat restrictions, embargoes and warfare, nearly ruining the fishing industry. Only with the fishing convention of 1818 did matters ease.

A source of wealth and of constant conflict, the cod fishery was wedded to our origins as a colony, to our birth as a nation and to our growth as a distinctive culture. Salt cod was a familiar food for generations of New Englanders, but that did not make it any easier to handle. Without batting an eye, Esther Howland informed the readers of her cookbook that they should soak the dried fish overnight, drain it and broil it brown before commencing the real work. "Put it on a board," she wrote, "and beat it with a pestle, or hammer, till it becomes entirely soft."

Ironically, the all-prolific cod, once thought inexhaustible, proved not to be as tough as the salted product. With the rise of factory fishing, even the massive populations on the Grand Banks began to decline and ultimately to crash. A single ship in the 1960s could catch and process as much fish in an hour as a ship of the 1660s could in an entire season. In 1994, over a chorus of protest from New England fisherman, the Magnuson Fishery Conservation and Management Act of 1976 was amended, severely curtailing the catch in the hopes of making it sustainable. The fishing industry in New England collapsed, and it has never fully recovered. The Sacred Cod still hangs, more memory now than regent.

Clams

Were one to turn back the clock to the nineteenth century, the thought of clams dancing in the sand might well have set off a nostalgic reverie, reminding us of the natural bounty of our New England. It might have evoked warm thoughts of our hardy

Puritan forebears and their resilience in building a new society and of what they had learned from the Indians during those early and fitful winters. New Englanders were beginning to imagine the clam as part of their heritage. When the Puritans arrived, we might have said, clams and oysters abounded in the mudflats of settlements like Agawam (Ipswich), and they became one of the reliable sources of sustenance for the new settlers. The "Pilgrims to Plymouth," wrote the "Boston Housekeeper" N.K.M. Lee, "could cook this shell fish and lobsters in nearly fifty different ways, and even as puddings, pancakes, &c." They were inventive, adventurous and adaptable, all while dressed in drab.

If only it were so simple. Today, clams may have overtaken fish as the most popular protein in chowder, but they have done so by reversing a dubious early status. In Britain, shellfish were regionally popular—cockles were collected by Welsh women for centuries, and oysters carried a high-class cachet—but clams were typically considered fit only for the poor or for times of famine and privation. Early New England settlers showed little love for them, even as they noted how abundant they were in the tidal flats and how important they were to the Indian diet. Harvested in winter by Indian women, clams were consumed in such great quantities that most coastal Indian villages were marked by massive shell middens. Clam shells were used to make hoe blades (a woman's implement), spoons and scrapers and were one of the sources of wampum, the shell beads that were strung into strings and belts for sacred use in treaty making and that were used as currency in exchanges with the English. For Indians, the clam was more than a seasonal meal.

William Wood, an early promoter of New England emigration, remarked that everywhere the English looked upon their arrival, they found shellfish. Mussels were prolific but of inferior quality to the English variety, he noted, and were "left only for the hogs," while the equally plentiful clams were also "a great commodity

Postcard of a soft-shell clam from Plymouth, Massachusetts. In chowders, steamers today are most likely to be found in Maine. *Courtesy of the New England Chowder Compendium.*

for the feeding of swine, both in winter and summer; for being once used to those places, they [the swine] will repair to them as duly at every ebb as if they were driven to them by keepers." Ever resourceful, pigs returned over and over to rob the Indian clam grounds. "In some places of the country there be Clams as big as a penny white loaf," Wood noted, "which are great dainties amongst the natives, and would be in good esteem amongst the English, were it not for better fish." For the English, if not their pigs, the clam was merely a grudging meal.

What struck Wood and other English observers about the Indian use of shellfish was that the labor to gather them was provided by women, and Wood lambasted Indians for their cockeyed (or cockle-eyed?) division of labor between men and women. Indian men, he wrote, showed that they were inherently lazy, spending their days hunting and socializing while women did the hard work of farming and gathering food. Indian men "keep no set meals," he noted, but when they run out of stores, "they champ on the bit, till they meet with fresh supplies, either from their own endeavours, or their wives industry, who trudge to the clam-banks when all other means fail." To many observers from the time of English settlement until well into the nineteenth century, this male laziness and "abuse" of women was prima facie evidence of the lesser state of Indian civilization and reinforced the idea that Indian use of land was inefficient and underproductive. Hog food, women's work and Indian associations did not help the reputation of the humble clam.

And yet clams sustained the English settlers through hard times. During the lean year of 1623, William Bradford complained that the "best dish" to be found in the Plymouth colony was "a lobster or a piece of fish without bread or anything else but a cup of fair spring water," while during the grain shortage of 1631, the colony's women were reduced to gathering mussels to stay alive. Looking back on this history in 1760, Thomas Hutchinson wrote that the settlers "were so short of provisions" in those years "that they were obliged to live upon clams, mussels and other shell-fish, with ground-nuts and acorns instead of bread" (a typical Indian meal, in other words). Providence, however, famously intervened. "A good man, who had asked his neighbour to a dish of clams," Hutchinson wrote, sent a prayer of thanks to God for "the abundance of the seas and of treasure hid in the sands." Having set aside February 22 as a day of fast, the good man's prayer was answered on the fifth, when the ship *Lyon* arrived laden with provisions, turning the fast into thanksgiving.

For some at least, clams were more than just a godsend or stopgap to starvation. They may have been less relished than meat (beef, pork and lamb), and may have been food for the lower strata of society, but they were not ignored. Oysters and other shellfish were valued not only for their nutritive value but also for the lime that could be extracted from their shells. In 1745, the Rhode Island Assembly enacted a law to preserve oyster beds

Three clammers on the Essex River, Essex, Massachusetts, November 15, 1907. *A Report from the Mollusk Fisheries of Massachusetts (1909).*

from "evil minded Persons" and to prevent the "evil Practice of burning said Shell Fish into Lime, or otherwise to destroy the same." Clams may not ever have been as favored as oysters, but they, too, were considered appropriate for protection. In 1787, Massachusetts passed an act to preserve the oyster beds on Cape Cod against people who would rake the beds clean of oysters and "other useful shell fish," thus contributing "to the great damage of the poor and other inhabitants." The legislature was serious enough that it prohibited anyone from carrying more than three bushels at a time, "including the shells." Poor relief, one of the responsibilities of town governments, could take many forms.

A few writers suggest that clams were consumed more eagerly than is commonly supposed in the eighteenth century, with their appeal perhaps growing with the passage of time and tastes. In 1743, the English author of the *History and Present State of the British Islands* defended his native cuisine against the scorn of a French writer by complaining that the Frenchman had omitted "a great deal of our best Food, such as Sea and River Fish of all kinds, which dress'd with Oysters, Shrimps, and rich Sauces" were as good as any French dish. Furthermore, the complainant had ignored English "Venison, Game and Wild-fowl, Westphalia Hams, Lamb in the depth of Winter, Lobsters and other Shell-fish, which are not uncommon at the Tables of our Gentlemen or Citizens, [and] will be allow'd equal perhaps to the most delicious French Morsels." Lobsters and clams may not have attained a gourmet status, and they may not have been consumed in great quantities, but they were nevertheless found on the tables of respectable men and could be enumerated among the "best foods." On this side of the Atlantic, the naturalist William Bartram cooed over the oyster-filled bays and the crabs and shrimp that proliferated off the coast of Georgia and Florida and singled out the clams for special note as being particularly "large, their meat white, tender, and delicate." Benjamin Lincoln considered the counties of eastern Maine blessed with "great advantages...from the shell-fish, viz. the lobster, the scollop, and the clam."

According to Keith Stavely and Kathleen Fitzgerald, the re-clam-ation project for clams began at some point after about 1700, and it was more than a century before clams were fully accepted. At the centennial celebration of the Plymouth landing in 1720, the celebratory meal commenced with a wooden bowl of maize and clams to signify the meager diet of the first settlers, after which a sumptuous dinner of New England's bounties pointed to how far the colony had come. A generation later with the founding of the Plymouth Old Colony Club and the Forefather's Day banquet, clams were served as part of a commemorative feast, not a symbol of privation any longer but of the abundance that fed our forefathers, symbols of "bounty and celebration." Clams entered the cuisine in soups, stews, pies, fritters and eventually chowder, and they were roasted, boiled or steamed, though well into the nineteenth century, they were still, in some quarters, considered a "plebeian dish, from which many persons turned in disgust."

More even than fish, clams required an effective means of preservation before they could be transformed into a marketable commodity on a commercial scale. After all, a bad clam is not easily forgotten. Oysters, the highest-value shellfish of the day, became wildly popular and were sent to saloons and taverns hundreds of miles inland, packed on ice and specially transported by river or road, but the lower-value clams never merited such treatment. Indeed, until late in the nineteenth century, clams were used more for fish bait than food. Most of the fresh-shucked trade went to bait for inshore fishermen, with steamed-out meats, salted and packed in barrels and sent to supply offshore fisherman, including those on the Grand Banks. Of the thirty-five thousand bushels of clams harvested at Chatham, Massachusetts, in 1880,

Bill for services as clam warden (May 5, 1925). *Courtesy of the Local History Room, Kingston Public Library.*

Sandra Oliver notes, only twenty-six hundred were eaten as food; the rest went into the mouths of cod. With fresh clams having a limited range and salting not a favorable option, to feed people would require a different method.

War and violence once again became the template on which chowder would be fashioned. With the French army engaged in wars in Europe, Africa, Asia and the Americas in 1795, and with its supply lines stretched to the limit, the French government faced a desperate need for a more reliable method for preserving food than drying, salting and pickling. More palatable would be a bonus. Despite the offer of a 12,000-franc premium to encourage innovation, it took years before the desired results were achieved. In 1809, the confectioner and caterer Nicolas Appert developed a process in which foods were sealed in airtight glass containers and sterilized, and although there was no theory of germs to explain why the process worked, it worked nevertheless. A year later, the English merchant Peter Durand improved on Appert's idea, patenting the process of preserving "animal, vegetable and other perishable foods in vessels of glass, pottery, tin or any fit materials." His genius was to realize that the container mattered: glass was too fragile and iron rusted. Durand therefore lit upon the idea of plating his iron cans with tin, which neither rusted nor degraded in water. Hosannas to the tin can and to Durand's successor, Bryan Donkin, who subsequently made a killing by supplying large quantities of canned meat to the Royal Navy.

Commercial canning operations quickly followed, with the first established in England by Donkin and John Hall in 1813 and in the United States at about the same time by Robert Ayars (although some reports attribute the first cannery to Thomas Kensett a few years later). Among the first products canned on a commercial scale in this country were the old problem children for food spoilage: fish and shellfish. By the 1840s, Baltimore had captured the bulk of the canned oyster trade thanks to the famous quality of the Chesapeake oyster beds, and the first lobster cannery was opened in Eastport, Maine, in 1843, giving a boost to a shellfish that was still considered suitable primarily for cheap eats. Demand for canned seafood rose relatively slowly until the Civil War, when military necessity once again kicked the can into high gear. With the return home of thousands of soldiers with firsthand experience with canned goods, the industry was primed for a peacetime boom.

Just as the war was ending in 1865, James Harvey Doxsee established the Doxsee Clam and Seafood Canning Company at Islip, Long Island, becoming a significant producer of canned clam chowder, chopped clams and clam juice. Like the owners of many other canning operations, Doxsee had to adjust as

The William Underwood Cannery for clam juice, chowder, lobster and mackerel (1891). *Courtesy of the Gulf of Maine Cod Project, NOAA National Marine Sanctuaries, National Archives.*

local stocks declined as a result of overfishing. One of his sons formed an independent ocean-fishing operation that continues to operate to this day, but Doxsee's operations shifted to North Carolina and then to Florida to be near a reliable supply. By the late 1870s, according to an article in the *Sydney Mail* on February 8, 1879, canneries in Canada were burgeoning, concentrating on lobster, fish, baked beans and clam chowder, as well as the latest novelty: fish balls. The canneries there, too, reported having to shift as the stocks of lobsters or fish rose or fell under the intense pressure of modern harvesting technologies, but as an industry, they faced a steadily increasing market. The rise in demand for canned foods, they speculated, was being driven by the rise in the number of people living in flats, leaving them little or no space for food preparation.

Maine became an epicenter of seafood canning. The first clam cannery there—sometimes said to be the first in the United States—may have been the firm of Burnham and Morrill, which built a plant at Pine Point in 1878. Credited with being the first to can corn, Burnham and Morrill produced a range of products—from fish to that other New England comfort food, B&M baked beans—but it was at the leading edge of a major industry. Demand was such that by the 1880s, there were twenty-three lobster canneries in Maine and nineteen corn canneries, with other operations canning produce and seafood in various combinations. The first efforts to can clams resulted in a discolored product, making for a ghastly consumer experience, but by the turn of the twentieth century, when Burnham and Morrill developed fish flakes, popular for use in chowders, canned clam chowder was being produced in canning centers from Maine to Maryland and soon on the West Coast. This most social dish entered the new century suitable for the bachelor, the loner, the renter and the rootless.

Conclusion

What, then, are we to make of chowder, born in conflict and steeped in a changing world? Canning and other developments may have began to erode the sociability that had long been central to the dish, and developments in the technology of fishing and fish processing may have begun to reshape our tastes, but as food historians Keith Stavely and Kathleen Fitzgerald point out, there is much more to be said in the way of perception. Chowder, they argue, "began to be seen in a sentimental light," not just as a humble food that fed the poor, but as a vestige of a treasured past that was fading away. The myths of the Indian origins of clamming and clambakes, the long-told stories of the ineffable knowledge of aging masters skilled in their arcane craft and the tales of the rough-hewn shipboard life and joyous chowder parties held on summery shores recalled a past that seemed increasingly distant to most Americans. "According to the formula for this type of story," Stavely and Fitzgerald argue, "these delicious chowders of old, like some magical dish once eaten upon an enchanted isle, were no longer to be had anywhere on earth."

First-class shore dinners: the Willow House in Quincy, Massachusetts. *Courtesy of the New England Chowder Compendium.*

To make sense of this nostalgic lament, to understand this remarkable reinvention of our past, it is important to recognize that its reinvention, like its invention, was part of something larger. In the decades between the 1880s and 1930s, many New Englanders—and many Americans more generally—rediscovered the value of a colonial past, imagined or real. The material life of the early years of our nation seemed to hold a new attraction for modern Americans, and a reverence for the seemingly decaying values of patriotism and democracy, for the moral life of community and family that our founders enjoyed, seemed suddenly vital and new. In architecture, where the revival was particularly pronounced, homes (almost always homes) were designed to echo colonial motifs, the restraint and symmetry of Georgian style playing out in restrained and symmetrical ways, but the colonial revival can be found in furniture and decorative arts as well, in plumbing fixtures and lighting, in literature, painting, and the collecting of antiquities and books. People like Wallace Nutting or the Allen sisters of Deerfield drew upon their colonial roots to make a handy living, purveying a vision of colonial lifestyle though photographs and artwork and the sale of meticulously-made reproduction furniture. Proponents of the colonial style were often passionate historical preservationists too: Colonial Williamsburg, Old Sturbridge Village and Mystic Seaport were arguably all offspring of the revival. Preserving the relics of the past, documenting and displaying them, replicating them, collecting and surrounding oneself with them, became all the rage.

It is easy to caricature the colonial revival as little more than nostalgia, but its effects on Americans were no less profound. It addressed a real desire, a need. After surviving the carnage of the Civil War and the tumult of national Reconstruction, Americans emerged into a cynical age inflamed by political corruption and the violent jousting of the power mad. Americans saw their nation swallowed up by a rising tide of social inequality and by the spasms of depression and economic distress. Americans witnessed unprecedented waves of immigration and emigration, industrialization and urbanization, and they stared down an unprecedented influx of new ideas, often "foreign" ideas, that left nothing secure in their wake, that left nothing in our hard-won republic to stand strong and enduring. It was as if the nation was unmasted and unmoored, drifting to the future uncharted.

This drift into a new type of nation that was mobile and competitive, rootless, amoral, and impersonal, could never be easy, but the colonial revival helped by anchoring us in a past (an imagined past) in which our nation was bonded in a common mission. Beleaguered by a sense of moral deterioration in their nation, as the historian T.J. Jackson Lears has suggested, Americans immersed themselves in the material past, in goods that represented a time when the nation had nurtured the family and social good. Rejecting the "decadent" excesses of high Victorian style and spurning the unnerving implications of industrialization and economic competition, the advocates of colonial revival favored simplicity and proportion and, as Karal Marling has written, they devoted themselves "to the regeneration of American virtue through the restoration of the American home." In an unreliable age, something as simple as a house, a painting, a chair, or lamp became more than just evidence of good taste, it became an emblem of our national ideals, a public expression of our deepest commitment to the values of a democratic heritage and our superiority as a nation. As the world roiled around us, we remained firm in our national vision, surrounded by our national past. Our American roots, as Dale Allen Gyure suggests, helped "ease the transition into the newness of the present and the uncertainty of the future."

Chowder was far from the most significant contributor to the colonial revival, but what it offered was the idea that a simple dish could survive in this modern world, connecting us to the values and practices of a stable and useful past. Chowder parties even offered the experience of a gathering on democratic principles, and even if bounded by the hours of an afternoon,

"Guardians of the Clam-Flats": a parade float in Kingston, Massachusetts, July 4, 1910. *Courtesy of the Local History Room, Kingston Public Library.*

they reinforced a sense of community and family. But like so many colonial revival reproductions, chowder could be machine made and "sentimentalization" aside, its contradictions were self-evident. One did not have to look hard to see that the fisheries were buckling under the impact of new and more efficient harvesting technologies, that community meant little in the shadow of America's dark Satanic mills, or that the newly emerging American culture had little patience for old ideas. Yet there chowder stood in its sturdy masculinity, evoking order and permanence, community and care. To insist on the authenticity of one or another recipe, even in the face of a profusion of chowder traditions, as many increasingly did, was to claim one's place in a would-be America and a stake in a particular democracy that was moral and social.

Ironically, such tangible connections to the past as chowder or colonial revival furniture involve as much forgetting as remembering, as much reinvention as preservation. The workingman's origins of the dish, the sometimes tragic histories of its ingredients, and the impact of modern life and modern technologies fade into nothingness in the grand search for authentic connection to a stable world. As a product of a seemingly simpler time wedded to the deep history of our economy and culture, as a

Above and next page: Advertisements for Davis Clam Chowder, Gloucester, Massachusetts (1919). *Courtesy of the New England Chowder Compendium.*

A pamphlet promoting the use of shellfish in American cooking. Tips for Cooking Fish and Shellfish, *U.S. Department of the Interior, Fish and Wildlife Service.*

set of ideas about masculinity and work and home, chowder was simply good to think about. From Harriet Beecher Stowe's yearning for the ante-railroad days and the Old Colony Club's celebration of the Plymouth Landing, the past had been useful for facing the present. It has always been so and will always be so. Chowder was comfort food, providing comfort that not all would be disturbingly new forever. Life was still as we knew it, still familiar. This was still New England.

Appendix A
Recipes

We lifted our voices and pronounced it "good."
—*L.W., 1867*

And such clam chowder as it was! Thick, juicy, succulent, it dripped down our throats like a sustaining nectar, some paradisal liquid that an angel must have evolved and mixed.
—*C.H. Towne, 1921*

DIET CLAM CHOWDER

A chowder that was unable to escape from emerging health fads of the 1970s.

4 ounces minced clams
1 cup skim milk
Onion flakes
Salt and pepper
Parsley flakes
Dash garlic powder
Butter flavoring or 1 teaspoon oleo

CHOWDER PATTIES

Leftover chowder is usually used to have another bowl. Mrs. Noah Avery had a new idea and decided to make some patties.

2 cups leftover chowder
1 egg
½ cup self-rising flour

Drain excess liquid. Mix all ingredients together. Form patties. Cook on greased baking sheet for 20 minutes at 500 degrees. Serve with dressing or ketchup.

CHOWDER, NEW ENGLAND

A chowder to be canned at home, published in the midst of World War II. "To prevent waste in the utilization of perishable food crops is important at any time, but it is absolutely essential when the conservation of food is vital to the national welfare."

9 cups chopped clam meat
1½ cups ground salt pork
1½ cups ground onion
½ cup flour
2 quarts clam juice
2 tablespoons salt
½ teaspoon white pepper
9 cups diced potato

Soft, hard or butter clams may be used. Clams should be thoroughly washed before shucking. Clams may be shucked raw or steamed open. In either case, the body membrane should be

A government pamphlet containing a recipe for canning chowder at home. Home Canning of Fishery Products, *U.S. Department of the Interior Conservation Bulletin 28. Issued November 1942. Reprinted November 1966.*

cut off, the siphon snipped off, the body cut open and the dark body mass removed.

Thoroughly wash the dressed meats and blanch them for 1 minute in boiling water that contains 2 tablespoons of salt and ¼ teaspoon of citric acid crystals to each quart. Drain the meats and chop them coarsely.

The juice should be saved when shucking raw clams. If the clams are steamed open, the juice may be caught in a pan placed beneath the steamer. Strain the juice and dilute it with water if the clam flavor is too strong.

Mix the pork and onions and cook them together in a kettle until they are soft and yellow. Beat the flour into the clam juice and add these to the pork and onions. Bring to a boil and add the seasoning. Thyme also may be used as seasoning if desired.

To prevent discoloration, blanch the potatoes immediately after dicing, or cover with water until needed.

Put ¾ cup of diced potato and ¾ cup of clam meat into each container, fill to the rim with hot soup and seal immediately.

Process: No. 2 cans 75 minutes and pint jars 80 minutes to 10 pounds of pressure (240 Fahrenheit). To prepare for the table, add an equal volume of milk to the canned chowder and bring to a boil. The recipe is sufficient to fill 12 No. 2 cans or pint jars.

Oven Fish Chowder

A chowder to be baked.

2 pounds cod or haddock
1 bay leaf
2 whole cloves
1 clove garlic minced
¼ cup butter
2 teaspoons pepper
4 potatoes, sliced
2 teaspoons salt
2 cups boiling water or stock
3 onions, sliced
½ cup dry white wine
1 tablespoon fresh parsley
2 cups light cream or milk

Put everything except cream into a casserole dish. Cover and bake at 375 degrees for one hour. Heat cream and add to chowder. Stir gently. Makes six to eight servings.

MUDDLE

New England muddles are closely linked to local chowder preparations. Here is one from the south shore of Massachusetts. Fish, milk and pork are present, but onions and potatoes are not.

> Fish Muddle (Mother's)
> 3 lbs (or less) of cod or haddock. Fry out a few slices of salt pork, add fish and water to nearly cover - Cook until fish is done (about 15 min.) Remove skin and bones and cover fish with milk (as much as you like) bring to boil - add salt and pepper to taste Thicken with a little flour (about 1 Tbsp. rubbed smooth with a little cold water

Fish muddle. *From the recipe box of C.T. Keith.*

REBUILDING A CHOWDER

This chowder was made over nineteen thousand days ago by a cook in his seventies. It was cooked in the twelfth year of the Cold War on a Thursday evening by the mouth of a small river. The sun set at 4:53 p.m. The temperature averaged thirty-five degrees.

A Kingston Yacht Club pennant.

Clam Chowder for Kingston Yacht Club   1/29/59

3 gals clams   with water to cover potatoes
6 lb onions   added made 14 gals
2 pks potatoes   Fed 90 men + women
2¾ lbs salt pork   3 gals left.
5 gals milk   Materials cost 40c a qt.
10 cans evap. milk   90 people consumed 88 pts
    Say 1pt per person.

4 box. Common crackers / 2 box left
5 " Crown pilots (2 " " /
3 qts mixed sw. pickles

Clam Chowder for Kingston Yacht Club. A recipe for ninety men and women, January 29, 1959. *From the recipe box of C.T. Keith.*

Notes for yacht club chowder, January 29, 1959. *From the recipe box of C. T. Keith.*

Shopping list for yacht club chowder, January 29, 1959. *From the recipe box of C. T. Keith.*

THREE CLAM CHOWDERS IN FOUR YEARS

1 qt. clams — Clam chowder
3 onions —
4 cups potatoe — 1 qt.
1½ tsp salt
⅛ tsp pepper
¼ lb fat pork.
2 qt milk — crackers
Serves 10

CLAM CHOWDER

4 qts. clams —
5 lb onions —
½ pk potatoes —
1 lb. fat pork —
6 qts milk —
3 cans Er. milk —
2 boxes Common crackers

Made chowder
to feed 30 men
with 2 quarts left over
10/18/48
used 12 onions
9 would be enough
1 Box common crackers
enough
¾ pk potatoes would
be better (no)

Above: Clam chowder. A serving for ten. *From the recipe box of C.T. Keith.*

Left: Clam chowder, October 18, 1948. A serving for thirty men. *From the recipe box of C.T. Keith.*

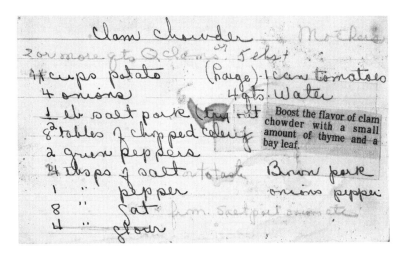

Clam chowder, December 15, 1952. A serving for twenty-two men. *From the recipe box of C.T. Keith.*

MOTHER'S CLAM CHOWDER

"Mother's Clam Chowder," a recipe from Connecticut featuring celery, peppers and tomatoes, circa 1925. *Courtesy of the R. Phillips Collection.*

Appendix B
Terms

ark of chowder: An alternative to the regular chowder festival.
Community members work to construct a large wooden bowl.
On the day of the celebration, local chowder makers come
together to pour in two pots each of their personal recipes.
In the words of Maine writer, Robert P.T. Coffin, "Give
everybody a stick. Let everybody stir. Too many cooks are the
making of the broth."

chowder festival: A celebration of chowder that rose to
popularity beginning in the early 1980s. While the chowder
parties of the past revolved around participation and
community building, the replacement can favor consumption
and competition.

common cracker: A dynamic chowder cracker. May also be
referred to as a "Boston" cracker. Approximately two and a
quarter inches wide. Can be split into halves, toasted, buttered
and floated on top of chowder.

deconstructed chowder: A chowder born out of an approach to food that rose to popularity in the 1990s and early 2000s. The chowder is broken down into its individual components and reimagined with new textures and new preparations.

junks: Another word for chunks. Also refers to the salted meat used as provisions aboard ships.

oyster cracker: Today, the most common chowder cracker. At restaurants, there are usually between fourteen and sixteen in a packet. For food writer M.F.K. Fisher, they were "light dead things." For their lovers, chowders can be reduced to a vehicle for the crackers.

pilot cracker: A big chowder cracker of approximately five inches. The G.H. Bent Company in Milton, Massachusetts, continues to produce its version, the Celebrated Pilot. Nabisco's Crown Pilot was discontinued in 2008. Residents of Chebeague Island, Maine, have been active in an effort for it to return.

quahog: *Mercenaria mercenaria*. A hard-shelled clam. The definitive clam for many southern New England chowders. Countnecks, littlenecks, cherrystones, top necks and quahogs refer to the same species but denote differences of size (from smallest to largest). The larger they become the less they are eaten raw.

salt pork: Pork back or pork belly cured with salt, sugar and nitrates.

Appendix C

Priscilla D. Webster versus the Blue Ship Tea Room

A transcript of an intriguing 1964 Massachusetts court case
involving a lawsuit with fish bones in a chowder.

Argued April 6, 1964.
Decided May 4, 1964.
347 Mass. 421, 198 N.E.2d 309. 2 UCC Rep.Serv. 161

*Action to recover for personal injuries sustained by reason of
alleged breach of implied warranty of merchantability of food
served by defendant in its restaurant. The defendant excepted to
the refusal of the trial judge to allow certain motions including
one to direct a verdict in its favor after a verdict for the plaintiff.*

*The Supreme Judicial Court, Reardon, J., held that no
chef is forced to reduce pieces of fish in chowder to miniscule
size in an effort to ascertain if they contain any pieces of bone,
and a fish bone lurking in fish chowder, about the ingredients
of which there is no other complaint, does not constitute a
breach of implied warranty under Uniform Commercial Code.*

Appendix C

Exceptions sustained.
Judgment for defendant.

John J.C. Herlihy, Neil L. Lynch, Boston, for defendant.
Blair L. Perry, Boston, for plaintiff.
Before WILKINS, C.J., and SPALDING, WHITTEMORE,
CUTTER and REARDON, JJ.

REARDON, Justice.

*This is a case which by its nature evokes earnest study not
only of the law but also of the culinary traditions of the
Commonwealth which bear so heavily upon its outcome. It is
an action to recover damages for personal injuries sustained by
reason of a breach of implied warranty of food served by the
defendant in its restaurant. An auditor, whose findings of fact
were not to be final, found for the plaintiff. On a retrial in the
Superior Court before a judge and jury, in which the plaintiff
testified, the jury returned a verdict for her. The defendant
is here on exceptions to the refusal of the judge (1) to strike
certain portions of the auditor's report, (2) to direct a verdict
for the defendant, and (3) to allow the defendant's motion for
the entry of a verdict in its favor under leave reserved.*

*The jury could have found the following facts: On Saturday,
April 25, 1959, about 1 P.M., the plaintiff, accompanied
by her sister and her aunt, entered the Blue Ship Tea Room
operated by the defendant. The group was seated at a table and
supplied with menus.*

*This restaurant, which the plaintiff characterized as
"quaint," was located in Boston "on the third floor of an old
building on T Wharf which overlooks the ocean."*

*The plaintiff, who had been born and brought up in New
England (a fact of some consequence), ordered clam chowder*

106

and crabmeat salad. Within a few minutes she received tidings to the effect that "there was no more clam chowder," whereupon she ordered a cup of fish chowder. Presently, there was set before her "a small bowl of fish chowder." She had previously enjoyed a breakfast about 9 A.M. which had given her no difficulty. "The fish chowder contained haddock, potatoes, milk, water and seasoning. The chowder was milky in color and not clear. The haddock and potatoes were in chunks" (also a fact of consequence). She agitated it a little with the spoon and observed that it was a fairly full bowl. It was hot when she got it, but she did not tip it with her spoon because it was hot, but stirred it in an up and under motion. She denied that she did this because she was looking for something, but it was rather because she wanted an even distribution of fish and potatoes. She started to eat it, alternating between the chowder and crackers which were on the table with [some] rolls. She ate about 3 or 4 spoonfuls then stopped. She looked at the spoonfuls as she was eating. She saw equal parts of liquid, potato and fish as she spooned it into her mouth. She did not see anything unusual about it. After 3 or 4 spoonfuls she was aware that something had lodged in her throat because she couldn't swallow and couldn't clear her throat by gulping and she could feel it. This misadventure led to two esophagoscopies at the Massachusetts General Hospital, in the second of which, on April 27, 1959, a fish bone was found and removed.

The sequence of events produced injury to the plaintiff which was not insubstantial. We must decide whether a fish bone lurking in a fish chowder, about the ingredients of which there is no other complaint, constitutes a breach of implied warranty under applicable provisions of the Uniform Commercial Code,[1] the annotations to which are not helpful on this point. As the judge put it in his charge, "Was the fish chowder fit to be eaten and wholesome?" [N]obody is claiming that the fish itself wasn't wholesome. But the bone of contention here—I don't mean that for a pun—was this fish bone a foreign substance that made the fish chowder unwholesome or not fit to be eaten?

The plaintiff has vigorously reminded us of the high standards imposed by this court where the sale of food is involved (see Flynn v. First Natl. Stores Inc., *296 Mass. 521, 523, 6 N.E.2d 814) and has made reference to cases involving stones in beans (*Friend v. Childs Dining Hall Co., *231 Mass. 65, 120 N.E. 407, 5 A.L.R. 1100), trichinae in pork (*Holt v. Mann, *294 Mass. 21, 22, 200 N.E. 403), and to certain other cases, here and elsewhere, serving to bolster her contention of breach of warranty.*

The defendant asserts that here was a native New Englander eating fish chowder in a "quaint" Boston dining place where she had been before; that "[f]ish chowder, as it is served and enjoyed by New Englanders, is a hearty dish, originally designed to satisfy the appetites of our seamen and fishermen"; that "[t]his court knows well that we are not talking of some insipid broth as is customarily served to convalescents." We are asked to rule in such fashion that no chef is forced "to reduce the pieces of fish in the chowder to miniscule size in an effort to ascertain if they contained any pieces of bone." "In so ruling," we are told (in the defendant's brief), "the court will not only uphold its reputation for legal knowledge and acumen, but will, as loyal sons of Massachusetts, save our world-renowned fish chowder from degenerating into an insipid broth containing the mere essence of its former stature as a culinary masterpiece." Notwithstanding these passionate entreaties we are bound to examine with detachment the nature of fish chowder and what might happen to it under varying interpretations of the Uniform Commercial Code.

Chowder is an ancient dish preexisting even "the appetites of our seamen and fishermen." It was perhaps the common ancestor of the "more refined cream soups, purees, and bisques." Berolzheimer, The American Woman's Cook Book *(Publisher's Guild Inc., New York, 1941) p. 176. The word "chowder" comes from the French "chaudiere," meaning a "cauldron" or "pot." In the fishing villages of Brittany "faire la chaudiere" means to "supply a cauldron in which is cooked a mess of fish and biscuit with some savoury condiments, a hodge-podge contributed by the fishermen themselves, each of whom in return receives his share of the prepared dish. The Breton fishermen probably carried the custom to Newfoundland, long famous for its chowder, whence it has spread to Nova Scotia, New Brunswick, and New England."* A New English Dictionary *(MacMillan and Co., 1893) p. 386. Our literature over the years abounds in references not only to the delights of chowder but also to its manufacture. A namesake of the plaintiff, Daniel Webster, had a recipe for fish chowder which has survived into a number of modern cookbooks[2] and in which the removal of fish bones is not mentioned at all. One old time recipe recited in the* New English Dictionary *study defines chowder as "A dish made of fresh fish (esp. cod) or clams, stewed with slices of pork or bacon, onions, and biscuit. Cider and champagne are sometimes added." Hawthorne, in* The House of the Seven Gables *(Allyn and Bacon, Boston, 1957) p. 8, speaks of "[a] codfish of sixty pounds, caught in the bay, [which] had been dissolved into the rich liquid of a chowder." A chowder variant, cod "Muddle," was made in Plymouth in the 1890s by taking "a three or four pound codfish, head added. Season with salt and pepper and boil in just enough water to keep from burning. When cooked, add milk and piece of butter."[3] The recitation of these ancient formulae suffices to indicate that in the construction of chowders in these parts in other years, worries about fish bones played no role whatsoever.*

This broad outlook on chowders has persisted in more modern cookbooks. "The chowder of today is much the same as the old chowder." The American Woman's Cook Book, *supra, p. 176. The all embracing Fannie Farmer states in a portion of her recipe, fish chowder is made with a "fish skinned, but head and tail left on. Cut off head and tail and remove fish from backbone. Cut fish in 2-inch pieces and set aside. Put head, tail, and backbone broken in pieces, in stewpan; add 2 cups cold water and bring slowly to boiling point. The liquor thus produced from the bones is added to the balance of the chowder."* Farmer, The Boston Cooking School Cook Book *(Little Brown Co., 1937) p. 166.*

*Thus, we consider a dish which for many long years, if well made, has been made generally as outlined above. It is not too much to say that a person sitting down in New England to consume a good New England fish chowder embarks on a gustatory adventure which may entail the removal of some fish bones from his bowl as he proceeds. We are not inclined to tamper with age old recipes by any amendment reflecting the plaintiff's view of the effect of the Uniform Commercial Code upon them. We are aware of the heavy body of case law involving foreign substances in food, but we sense a strong distinction between them and those relative to unwholesomeness of the food itself, e.g., tainted mackerel (*Smith v. Gerrish, 256 Mass. 183, 152 N.E. 318*), and a fish bone in a fish chowder. Certain Massachusetts cooks might cavil at the ingredients contained in the chowder in this case in that it lacked the heartening lift of salt pork. In any event, we consider that the joys of life in New England include the ready availability of fresh fish chowder. We should be prepared to cope with the hazards of fish bones, the occasional presence of which in chowders is, it seems to us, to be anticipated, and which, in the light of a hallowed tradition, do not impair* *their fitness or merchantability. While we are bouyed up in this conclusion by* Shapiro v. Hotel Statler Corp., *132 F.Supp. 891 (S.D.Cal.), in which the bone which afflicted the plaintiff appeared in "Hot Barquette of Seafood Mornay," we know that the United States District Court of Southern California, situated as are we upon a coast, might be expected to share our views. We are most impressed, however, by* Allen v. Grafton, *170 Ohio St. 249, 164 N.E.2d 167, where in Ohio, the Midwest, in a case where the plaintiff was injured by a piece of oyster shell in an order of fried oysters, Mr. Justice Taft (now Chief Justice) in a majority opinion held that "the possible presence of a piece of oyster shell in or attached to an oyster is so well known to anyone who eats oysters that we can say as a matter of law that one who eats oysters can reasonably anticipate and guard against eating such a piece of shell." (P. 259 of 170 Ohio St., p. 174 of 164 N.E.2d.)*

Thus, while we sympathize with the plaintiff who has suffered a peculiarly New England injury, the order must be:

Exceptions sustained.
Judgment for the defendant.

Notes

1. Unless excluded or modified by section 2-316, a warranty that the goods shall be merchantable is implied in a contract for their sale if the seller is a merchant with respect to goods of that kind. Under this section the serving for value of food or drink to be consumed either on the premises or elsewhere is a sale. (2) Goods to be merchantable must at least be such as (c) are fit for the ordinary purposes for which such goods are used. G.L. c. 106, S 2-314. (3)(b) [W]hen the buyer before entering into the contract has examined the goods or the sample or model as fully as he desired or has refused to examine the

goods there is no implied warranty with regard to defects which an examination ought in the circumstances to have revealed to him. G.L. c. 106, S 2-316.
2. "Take a cod of ten pounds, well cleaned, leaving on the skin. Cut into pieces one and a half pounds thick, preserving the head whole. Take one and a half pounds of clear, fat salt pork, cut in thin slices. Do the same with twelve potatoes. Take the largest pot you have. Fry out the pork first, then take out the pieces of pork, leaving in the drippings. Add to that three parts of water, a layer of fish, so as to cover the bottom of the pot; next a layer of potatoes, then two tablespoons of salt, 1 teaspoon of pepper, then the pork, another layer of fish, and the remainder of the potatoes. Fill the pot with water to cover the ingredients. Put over a good fire. Let the chowder boil twenty-five minutes. When this is done have a quart of boiling milk ready, and ten hard crackers split and dipped in cold water. Add milk and crackers. Let the whole boil five minutes. The chowder is then ready to be first-rate if you have followed the directions. An onion may be added if you like the flavor." "This chowder," he adds, *"is suitable for a large fishing party."* Wolcott, The Yankee Cook Book *(Coward-McCann, Inc., New York City, 1939) p. 9.*
3. Atwood, Receipts for Cooking Fish *(Avery & Doten, Plymouth, 1896) p. 8.*

Appendix D
Stories

His omnipresent mentor, the sea, is at hand to correct, gnawing, and rounding and moulding with busy teeth and fingers, till the sharp corners are made smooth and the gaudy tints softened and the sea's great aim is once more attained—the reduction off all with which it comes in contact to a gray in color and to a curve in form.
—Guy Whetmore Carryl, 1909

THE OLD ONE

Details of a chowder party from the *Weekly Magazine*, August 18, 1798:

> *Newbury-Port is about three miles from the sea. The inhabitants cheerfully devote a day to the entertainment of strangers, and this complaisance was experienced by our company. We were invited to sail down the Merrimack river to the Black Rocks. Here we landed some of our company, who preferred the sport of the meadows, while we proceeded*

in quest of fish. Though the time of tide was unfavourable, we catched a sufficient quantity of flounder, cod, and other fish, of which there is a great variety in this river. The two former, however, were preferred by the connoisseurs. About noon we landed; and being joined by the gunners, formed a party of about fifteen persons. None were idle: all were cooks. While some were employed in cleaning the fish, others were busied in peeling onions; till at length a large pot of victuals was prepared. They called it Chouder. I have no fondness for culinery researches: yet as this process was somewhat singular, it may not be improper to describe it.

Chouder may be made of any good fish; but the ingredients of our mess were as follow:
1. A few slices of the fattest pork,
2. A layer of flounders,
3. Ditto of onions,
4. Ditto of cod-fish,
5. Ditto of biscuit.

Then came the pork again, and the other articles in succession, till the pot was filled to the brim. Pepper, salt, and other seasoning, were liberally used. Being hung over the fire, without any water, for half an hour, it was then taken off the oar, from which it had been suspended, and which rested upon two jagged points of the rocks. We now formed a circle, and attended to the ceremony of saying grace, which is religiously adhered to in New England. The chouder was then put into large white shells, which we found on the beach, and we began to eat it with smaller shells, fastened to pieces of split shingle. These natural utensils answered every purpose of dishes and spoons. Our seats were the rocks. The breezes from the salt water, the exercise of the morning, and the length of time since breakfast, enabled us to do ample justice to chouder. Whether it was owing to an extraordinary appetite, or some peculiar excellence in our cheer, I shall not pretend to determine; but never did I taste anything so grateful to the palate. The best of liquors were added to the repast, and our pleasures were heightened by the agreeableness of our company.

THE SCHOONER ONE

Like all kitchens in this world we do not speak of often, ones found in hospitals, prisons and nursing homes—kitchens supporting struggles, not luxuries—the ship's galley is unknown as a place of creativity. The stories of sea cooks are told in silence. As jobs on land merge the activities of work and play, structure still guides the habits of those on the water. A new port and new food may be days away. There is an old saying sometimes used in reference to meals on the ocean: "God brings the ingredients, but the devil brings the cook." If the sentiment is true, it was not in the fall of 2010 aboard the *Westward*, a 125-foot schooner from Maine.

On a wet morning I awoke in Mystic. Shifting bodies came out from the bunks. Whispers were the alarms. The smell of breakfast came down the hall. The crew was stirring. The cook was cooking. The first plastic mugs of coffee were filled. We climbed up the stairs to the deck. The light was still gray, and the sun was still coming. Omelets and pancakes were on the table. We went under and sat down. On the shelf behind us was a book of charts. It caught my attention as I ate. The orange juice passed across the table. It would take time to get out of this harbor.

Cooking at sea has never been easy. The cook balances to movements of the ocean. She or he is attentive to nuances brought by the wind and shifting sails. Even when the boat is steaming, the process may be difficult. Flames and pots come at odd angles. Today, a galley is better secured to help ease these tensions but it only takes one swell to send pans flying. Cutting boards have their own brackets. Bowls and mugs are kept in cabinets tied shut. The coffee pots sit in cutouts.

We motored out of the harbor, and the sails went up. Already, lunch was being planned, a chowder for twelve. The stove and burners were located midship. Around the time of the first chowders, three essentials: flint, steel and char cloth, together a tinderbox, appear to be suspects for firing up the first pots. The first two, when struck, release tiny sparks of iron; in combustion, they ignite the third—woven fabric of vegetable fiber. Here, every morning, a member of the crew ignited diesel with a lighter.

The second mate put a long line out to trawl for fish. A few minutes passed, and there was one flapping on the deck. It was filleted and cut into small pieces and eaten raw. The rest went down below and into the chowder pot. The smell of bacon and onions drifted through the holes in the boat. "Like fishes dreaming of the sea, and waking in the spider," wrote a poet. The cook sent me to get more ingredients in the reefer. Cold corn, tuna steaks and shrimp all went in. The fresh dairy was gone, but hiding in the chest under the cushions in the salon were cans of evaporated milk. I brought them to her. The chowder cooked, and the chowder finished.

Climbing up the steps with a bowl, broth fell over the sides. I took a seat on a box of lifejackets. I looked across the bay. The sky glowed in a four-mile radius around us. It swept over us to the other sides to feel the shape of the earth. Smoke from a cigar ran across the deck and went overboard. It climbed in the air, around the mast and into the sails. At forty feet it looked down. It saw us and the tops of our heads and on the last spoonful of our chowder it disappeared with our conversations. We wiped down the table and did dishes. I went to bed and awoke three hours later for a watch. The angle of the bow was high out of the water. It denied the horizon. At 10:30 at night we were heading for the moon. Chowder and the future were somewhere there on the mind.

THE LAST ONE

He was old and told you he would make you chowder.

The temperature is forty degrees, and clouds are moving to the northeast. A prism in the deck is trying to capture the sun. In a kitchen under the floor, a cook is holding his hands under a faucet. He closes his eyes. He sees his father in a diner by the corner at the lights. They sit and have pot pie and talk for hours. He walks out the door, and bells shake on the glass. He isn't in the street. He's at sea in the dark.

The pot on the stove is frying little onions, fat bubbles up around pieces of pork and potatoes boil to good temperatures. Two dozen clams are untied from bundles of newspaper. They are damp and are running stories with the Kennedys. They are put on handfuls of flowers taken at night from far back in the salt meadows. He chops them quickly, and juices splash over his hands and soak his shirt. It all runs across the cutting board and picks up the colors of the petals. He cries. He crushes herbs. He wipes his eyes. He wipes the knife, and everything is in the pot. The onions are gone, and they are now ghosts.

He wrings out what is left in his clothes and pours in milk: similar to stuff made by Melville's cow. The cow eats pieces of dying cods and haddocks arriving daily on the beach. It lactates with hesitation. It wants privacy.

The smell is an ocean and a problem. It spreads up the hills and wakes up women and men from deep winter sleep and pulls them to the shoreline wrapped in blankets. They mingle and chat and take pictures with new cameras and wait in lines for opportunities to tap the cow's potential. An annual event. A sacrilege. Watercolors will be made as new ways for remembering.

There is smoke in the distance, cedar wood burning and rising from a chimney. The chowder is coming off the burner, and all the smells meet up and are sweet in the air. He pounds some crackers into the counter. He documents the meal. He presses his finger into wax warming by the burner. He stamps it with a fresh date: his 1,200[th] chowder. Thousands of thin blocks line the boat from the bow to the sleeping quarters in the stern. They tell of different meals and different ingredients—of takeout food, hot toddies and pancakes. Now it is time to eat. There is no fog. The sun has gone under the horizon. It flashes green, disappears.

Bibliography

Adams, Harriet, and N.M. Halper. *Vittles for the Captain: Cape-Cod Sea-Food Recipes*. Provincetown, MA: Modern Pilgrim Press, 1941.

Anderson, Virginia DeJohn. *Creatures of Empire: How Domestic Animals Transformed Early America*. New York: Oxford, 2004.

Armstrong, Maurice W. "The Diary of Caleb Gannet for the Year 1776." *William and Mary Quarterly* 3, no. 1 (1946).

Atkinson, Joseph. *A Match for a Widow: or, The Frolics of Fancy. A Comic Opera, in Three Acts*. Dublin: P. Byrne, 1788.

Bartram, William. *Travels through North and South Carolina, Georgia, East and West Florida, the Cherokee Country, the Extensive Territories of the Muscogulges, or Creek Confederacy, and the Country of the Chactaws*. Philadelphia: James and Johnson, 1791.

Beecher, Catherine E. *Miss Beecher's Domestic Receipt-Book, Designed as a Supplement to Her Treatise on Domestic Economy*. 3rd ed. New York: Harper and Brothers, 1850.

Beecher, Catherine E., and Harriet Beecher Stowe. *The American Woman's Home*. New York: J.B. Ford & Co., 1869.

Boys, William. *An Account of the Loss of the* Luxborough *Galley, by Fire, on Her Voyage from Jamaica to London: with the Sufferings of Her crew, in the Year 1727.* London, 1787.

Briggs, Richard. *The English Art of Cookery, According to the Present Practice.* London: G.G. and J. Robinson, 1794.

Carew, Bampfylde-Moore. *The Life and Adventures of Bampfylde-Moore Carew, the Noted Devonshire Stroller and Dog-Stealer.* Exon: The Farleys, 1745.

Carter, Susannah. *The Frugal Housewife, Or, Complete Woman Cook.* New York: G. & R. Waite, 1803.

Child, Lydia Maria. *The American Frugal Housewife, Dedicated to Those Who Are Not Ashamed of Economy.* 22nd ed. New York: Samuel S. and William Wood, 1838.

Coffin, Robert P. Tristram. *Mainstays of Maine,.* New York: Macmillan, 1944.

Corson, Juliet. *Miss Corson's Practical American Cookery and Household Management.* New York: Deed, Mead and Co., 1886.

Daughters of the American Revolution. *Cook Book.* Norwalk, CT, 1923.

Deutsch, Jonathan. "'Please Pass the Chicken Tits': Rethinking Men and Cooking at an Urban Firehouse." *Food and Foodways* 12 (2005): 91–114.

De Voe, Thomas F. *The Market Assistant: Containing a Brief Description of Every Article of Human Food Sold in the Public Markets of the Cities of New York, Boston, Philadelphia, and Brooklyn; Including the Various Domestic and Wild Animals, Poultry, Game, Fish, Vegetables, Fruits &c., &c. with Many Curious Incidents and Anecdotes.* Philadelphia: Hurd and Houghton, 1867.

Dyott, William. *Dyott's Diary, 1781–1845: A Selection from the Journal of William Dyott.* Edited by Reginald W. Jeffery. London: Archibald Constable, 1907.

Ellet, Elizabeth F. *The New Cyclopaedia of Domestic Economy, and Practical Housekeeper, Adapted to All Classes of Society.* Norwich, CT: Henry Bill, 1872.

Farmer, Fanny Merritt. *Boston Cooking-School Cookbook.* Boston: Little, Brown and Co., 1896.

Glasse, Hannah. *The Art of Cookery Made Plain and Easy.* 6th ed. London: A Millar, 1758.

Good Housekeeping Every Day Cook Book. N.p., 1903.

Gyure, Dale Allen. "The Colonial Revival: A Review of the Literature." In *Colonial Revival in America: Annotated Bibliography.* Edited by Karen L. Mulder. http://etext. virginia.edu/colonial.

Hale, Edward E. "How a Writer Should Live." *The Critic* 4 (1885).

The History and Present State of the British Islands. Vol. 1. London: Jacob Robinson, 1743.

Howland, Esther Allen. *The New England Economical Housekeeper, and Family Receipt Book.* Cincinnati, OH: H.W. Derby, 1845.

Hutchinson, Thomas. *The History of the Colony of Massachusetts-Bay.* London: M. Richardson, 1760.

Innis, Harold A. *The Cod Fisheries: The History of an International Economy.* New Haven, CT: Yale University Press, 1940.

Johnson, Charles. *A General History of Pyrates, From Their First Rise and Settlment in the Island of Providence, to the Present Time.* 2nd ed. London: T. Warner, 1724.

Knight, S.G. *Tit-Bits; Or, How to Prepare a Nice Dish at a Moderate Expense.* Boston: Crosby and Nichols, 1864.

Lear, W.H. "History of Fisheries in the Northwest Atlantic: A Five-Hundred-Year Perspective." *Journal of Northwest Atlantic Fishery Science* 23 (1998): 41–73.

Lears, T.J. Jackson. *No Place of Grace: Antimodernism and the Transformation of American Culture, 1880–1920.* Chicago: University of Chicago Press, 1981.

Lee, N.K.M. "Boston Housekeeper." *The Cook's Own Book, Being a Complete Culinary Encyclopedia*. Boston: Munroe and Francis, 1832.

Leslie, Eliza. *Miss Leslie's New Cookery Book*. Philadelphia: T.B. Peterson, 1857.

Lincoln, Benjamin. "Observations on the Climate, Soil and Value of the Eastern Counties in the District of Maine, Written in the Year 1789." *Collections of the Massachusetts Historical Society* 1 (1795).

Lincoln, Mary Johnson Bailey. *Mrs. Lincoln's Boston Cook Book: What to Do and What Not to Do in Cooking*. Boston: Roberts Brothers, 1896.

Livingston, James D. *Arsenic and Clam Chowder: Murder in Gilded Age New York*. Albany, NY: SUNY Press, 2010.

Madden, Etta M., and Martha L. Finch, eds. *Eating in Eden: Food and American Utopias*. Lincoln, NE: University of Nebraska, 2006.

Magra, Christopher Paul. "The New England Cod Fishing Industry and Maritime Dimensions of the American Revolution." PhD diss., University of Pittsburgh, 2006.

Marling, Karal Ann. George Washington Slept Here: Colonial Revivals and American Culture, 1876–1986. Cambridge, MA: Harvard University Press, 1988.

Neustadt, Kathy. Clambake: *A History and Celebration of an American Tradition*. Amherst: University of Massachusetts, 1992.

Oliver, Sandra L. *Saltwater Foodways: New Englanders and Their Food, At Sea and Ashore, in the Nineteenth Century*. Mystic, CT: Mystic Seaport Museum, 1995.

Parloa, Maria. *The Appledore Cook Book, Containing Practical Receipts for Plain and Rich Cooking*. Boston: Graves and Ellis, 1872.

Putnam, Elizabeth H. *Mrs. Putnams Receipt Book, and Young Housekeeper's Assistant*. New and enlarged edition. Boston: Ticknor, Reed and Fields, 1853.

Randolph, Mary. *The Virginia Housewife: or, Methodical Cook.* Baltimore, MD: Plaskitt & Cugel, 1838.

Reader, John. Potato: *A History of the Propitious Esculent.* New Haven, CT: Yale University Press, 2009.

The Re-Union of '73: The Second Reception of the Sons and Daughters of Portsmouth, Resident Abroad. Portsmouth, NH: C.W. Gardner, 1873.

Salaman, Redcliffe N. *The History and Social Influence of the Potato.* Cambridge, UK: Cambridge University Press, 1949.

Seneca (Henry H. Soule). *Canoe and Camp Cookery: A Practical Cookbook for Canoeists, Corinthian Sailors, and Outers.* New York: Forest and Stream, 1885.

Smollett, Tobias. *The Adventures of Sir Launcelot Greaves.* London: J. Coote, 1762.

———. *The Expedition of Humphry Clinker.* London: W. Johnson, 1771.

Stavely, Keith, and Kathleen Fitzgerald. *America's Founding Food: The Story of New England Cooking.* Chapel Hill: University of North Carolina Press, 2004.

Thoreau, Henry David. *Cape Cod.* New York: Houghton Mifflin, 1864.

Thorne, John. *Down East Chowder.* Boston: Jackdaw Press 1982.

Towne, Charles H. "Loafing Down Long Island." *The Century Illustrated Monthly Magazine* (1921).

W., L. "Nantucket: Up on the Walk, Island Peculiarities, The Town Crier, Ancient Customs, Antipathy to Trees, Nantucket Clam Chowder." *New York Times*, August 12, 1867.

Whetmore Carryl, Guy. "New England Fisher Folk." *Harper's Monthly Magazine* 105 (1902).

Whittier, John Greenleaf. *Margaret Smith's Journal ; Tales and Sketches.* Boston: Houghton, Mifflin, 1889.

Wood, William. *New-England's Prospect.* Boston: Thomas and John Fleet, 1764.

About the Authors

J acob Walker spends most of his time along the coast of Massachusetts. He is the creator of the New England Chowder Compendium, a nationally recognized project at the University of Massachusetts–Amherst devoted to examining all things chowder.

R ob Cox spends far too little time along the coast of Massachusetts. A former paleontologist and molecular biologist, he has a doctorate in history from the University of Michigan and works at the University of Massachusetts–Amherst. He is author of *Body and Soul: A Sympathetic History of American Spiritualism* (Charlottesville, 2003) and editor of and contributor to *The Shortest and Most Convenient Route: Lewis and Clark in Context* (Philadelphia, 2004).

A life preserver.
Courtesy of D.W.